Perspectives on Rethinking and Reforming Education

MW00861110

Series Editors

Zhongying Shi, Faculty of Education, Beijing Normal University, Beijing, China
Shengquan Yu, Faculty of Education, Beijing Normal University, Beijing, China

This book series brings together the latest insights and work regarding the future of education from a group of highly regarded scholars around the world. It is the first collection of interpretations from around the globe and contributes to the interdisciplinary and international discussions on possible future demands on our education system. It serves as a global forum for scholarly and professional debate on all aspects of future education. The book series proposes a total rethinking of how the whole education process can be reformed and restructured, including the main drivers and principles for reinventing schools in the global knowledge economy, models for designing smart learning environments at the institutional level, a new pedagogy and related curriculums for the 21st century, the transition to digital and situated learning resources, open educational resources and MOOCs, new approaches to cognition and neuroscience as well as the disruption of education sectors. The series provides an opportunity to publish reviews, issues of general significance to theory development, empirical data-intensive research and critical analysis innovation in educational practice. It provides a global perspective on the strengths and weaknesses inherent in the implementation of certain approaches to the future of education. It not only publishes empirical studies but also stimulates theoretical discussions and addresses practical implications. The volumes in this series are interdisciplinary in orientation, and provide a multiplicity of theoretical and practical perspectives. Each volume is dedicated to a specific theme in education and innovation, examining areas that are at the cutting edge of the field and are groundbreaking in nature. Written in an accessible style, this book series will appeal to researchers, policy-makers, scholars, professionals and practitioners working in the field of education.

More information about this series at http://www.springer.com/series/14177

Xudong Zhu · Jian Li

Classroom Culture in China

Collective Individualism Learning Model

 Springer

Xudong Zhu
Faculty of Education
Beijing Normal University
Beijing, China

Jian Li
Faculty of Education
Beijing Normal University
Beijing, China

ISSN 2366-1658   ISSN 2366-1666   (electronic)
Perspectives on Rethinking and Reforming Education
ISBN 978-981-15-1829-4   ISBN 978-981-15-1827-0   (eBook)
https://doi.org/10.1007/978-981-15-1827-0

This Springer imprint is published by the registered company Springer Nature Singapore Pte Ltd.
The registered company address is: 152 Beach Road, #21-01/04 Gateway East, Singapore 189721,
Singapore

Preface

This book fundamentally examines the idea of classroom culture in the Chinese context and creates the proposed model of "Collective Individualism Learning". The idea of classroom culture plays a fundamental role in constructing students' learning competencies, perceptions, and behaviors comprehensively. This book also conceptualizes and contextualizes the collective individualism learning model to explicate a specific learning model in classroom culture at a Chinese particular context historically and traditionally. The proposed collective individualism model is identified as the individualized learning style of students in Chinese classroom culture characterized by "nine symbolic objects", including a textbook, an exercise book, a pen, a blackboard, a screen, a computer, a table, a chair, and platform in a Chinese collective class. The two core components of formal collectivism and substantive individualism are derived from constructive learning theory, social learning theory, Mezirow's transformative learning theory, and Kolb's experiential learning theory. The implications for examining the collective individualism model of Chinese classroom culture are likewise linked to innovative talent cultivation and fulfillment of "Four Good Teachers" goal. Both the discussion and conclusion led to the construction of promising classroom culture in a Chinese context practically.

The idea of "Collective Individualism Learning" from contextual, conceptual, practical, and strategic scopes, especially for current Chinese education institutions to examine a learning model with Chinese characteristics, historically and traditionally. The summarized concept of "Collective Individualism Learning" has been constructed, examined, and discussed in the process of constructing classroom culture with Chinese characteristics. Specifically, the idea of collective individualism model is concluded as a personal learning style of students in specific classroom culture, including some particular symbolic objects. The constructive learning theory, social learning theory, Mezirow's transformative learning theory, and Kolb's experiential learning theory all contribute to investigate the classroom culture with Chinese characteristics. The implications for examining classroom culture are linked to realize the goal of "Four Good Teachers". Therefore, this book focuses on addressing the major leading issues on how to construct classroom culture by the means of "Collective Individualism Learning". Therefore, this book contributes to constructing the initial idea of "Collective Individualism Learning" for constructing classroom culture in Chinese higher education context. This innovative idea of "Collective Individualism Learning" tries to bring an in-depth understanding of the implicit connection between classroom culture and Chinese characteristics. The unique selling point could guarantee the unique attractions on the new conception of "Collective Individualism Learning" from conceptual, practical, and strategically dimensions.

The details of each chapter are illustrated as follows:

The introductory chapter involves examining the diverse and complex approach in which classroom culture contributes to the shaping of students' learning cultural identity. Classroom culture plays a fundamental role in constructing students' learning competencies, perceptions, and behaviors. Thus, this study conceptualizes and contextualizes a collective individualism learning model to explicate a specific learning model in classroom culture in the Chinese particular context historically and traditionally. The collective individualism model is identified as the individualized learning style of students in Chinese classroom culture characterized by nine symbolic objects, including a textbook, an exercise book, a pen, a blackboard, a screen, a computer, a table, a chair, and platform in a Chinese collective class. In addition, two core components of formal collectivism and substantive individualism derived from constructive learning theory, social learning theory, Mezirow's transformative learning theory, and Kolb's experiential learning theory. The implications for examining the collective individualism model of Chinese classroom culture are likewise linked to innovative talent cultivation and fulfillment of "Four Good Teachers" goal. Both the discussion and conclusion led to the construction of promising classroom culture in the Chinese context practically.

Chapter 2 concentrates on contextualizing "Collective Individualism Learning" from the perspective of Chinese model of classroom culture. It involves the introduction of classroom learning with Chinese characteristics, the material and cultural characteristics of "nine one" classrooms of collective individual learning, the connotative construction of collective individual learning, and the conclusion related to constructing collective individual learning model.

Chapter 3 involves puts forward the urgency and the necessity of construction of classroom culture, classroom culture problems lead to education reform cannot succeed, only transform the classroom culture can get rid of the plight of the education reform, classroom culture is the student studies the guaranteed rights culture, classroom culture is the most basic condition of students to learn effectively carried out; Second from students' physiological and physical development, cognitive and emotional development, moral and civic development, personality and sociality development, health and safety, the point of view of the needs of the development of art and aesthetic connotation of classroom culture building, and then discusses the promoting teachers' professional consciousness change and the transformation of the students to learn the value of classroom culture, finally proposed based on school culture, teachers'self-knowledge, discipline and study period, such as information technology classroom culture build path.

Chapter 4 explores offering the review of classroom culture from the studies on the Chinese context. It mainly involves the definitions of class culture, Chinese current studies on classroom culture, the construction of classroom culture, and the Chinese development stage of classroom culture research. All these sections contribute to analyzing the review of classroom culture from the studies of the Chinese context.

Chapter 5 concentrates on integrating classroom culture from the perspectives of core values of Chinese socialism. Specifically, the core value of socialism is an important part of socialism with Chinese characteristics in the new era. It is the dominant value or value system formed by the society under the socialist background. It is the core and foundation of the socialist value system. it concentrates on exploring the definition of China's socialist core values, development and cultivation of socialist core values, and the connotation of socialist core values. The influence of socialist core values and its significance to the education and cultivation of Adolescent Values.

Chapter 6 involves examining the relationship between classroom culture and Chinese traditional culture contextually. Introduction of classroom culture, the overview of campus culture, research contents of campus culture in China, review of Chinese studies on campus culture in Chinese context, the relationship between class culture and campus culture, and case studies on the relationship between class culture and campus culture all concentrate on figuring how to examine the relations between classroom culture and Chinese traditional culture, specifically.

Chapter 7 concentrates on exploring the relations between class culture and Chinese traditional culture. Class culture is an important part of school culture. Class culture shows a class's unique spiritual outlook, which affects students' thinking, cognition, and behavior, and dominates students' daily learning and life with a unique group reaction. Class culture represents the image of the class and reflects the life of the class. Class culture construction plays a key role in the development of the class.[1] The importance of class culture construction has been recognized more and more. Researchers began to actively explore new ideas of class culture construction. Some researchers have proposed to build class culture based on traditional Chinese culture. Then, how about the research on traditional culture and class culture? Therefore, this study combines the relationship between class culture and traditional culture, and how to build class culture based on traditional culture, in order to promote the further development of relevant research and practice.

Beijing, China   Xudong Zhu
                                                                                                          Jian Li

---

[1]Zhang Ying. Read the "Three-character Classic" Well to Cultivate New People—A Useful Exploration of Developing the Cultural Construction of Characteristic Classes [J]. Huaxia Teachers, 2015 (10):14–15.

Acknowledgements

In the realization of this book, we are grateful for the generosity and positive spirit of collegiality. We would like to express our appreciation to many experts and scholars to accept interviews to share their academic viewpoints and experiences in order to enrich the study of classroom culture contextually. We are really grateful for the generosity and positive spirit of collegiality. While most of the chapters in this book are original, several are adopted from my previously published material and the editors are grateful for the kind permissions granted to facilitate this.

Warmly Thanks To

Wangqian Fu is a post-doctor and assistant researcher at the China Institute of Education and Social Development, Beijing Normal University. She earned her doctoral degree in Beijing Normal University as well in 2019. Her research interests include education policy, inclusive education, and special education with research and publications on internationalization of higher education; the implication of inclusive education of U.S. to China; the education equality for the children with disabilities. She has been the Editor in charge of public opinion of education weekly, which is entrusted by the Ministry of Finance.

Contents

About the Authors

Xudong Zhu is the Dean of Faculty of Education and the Professor in the Institute of Teacher Education of Beijing Normal University. His work focuses on teacher education, comparative education, and history of education, with an emphasis on the system transformation of teacher education in China, a comparative study on the national development and education, the history of ideas of education in the West. Much of his work has involved the policy, practice of teacher education, and teacher professional development, supported by research in China, World Bank, UNESCO, Intel, etc. He is the Secretary of National Expert Committee of Teacher Education of MOE in China, the Director of the Center for Teacher Education Research among the Key Research Institutes of Humanities and Social Sciences in the University of MOE. He is Director of Institute of Teacher Education of Beijing Normal University, and an Editor-in-Chief of the Journal of Teacher Education Research, China. He was the Fulbright Senior Visiting Scholar of the U.S. State Department during the year 2002–2003.

Jian Li is the Assistant Professor at China Institute of Education and Social Development, Faculty of Education, Beijing Normal University. She received her Ph.D. in Educational Leadership and Policy Studies (ELPS), School of Education, Indiana University Bloomington, USA. Her research interests focus on Teacher Education, Global Learning, Global Competence, Global Citizenship, Globalization and Internationalization of Higher Education. She has also published a couple of English papers and monographs regarding the topics of soft power of higher education, the higher education with Chinese characteristics, global shared higher education communities, and faculty development in the Chinese context. Dr. Li currently also serves as think tanker at China Institute of Education and Social Development, Beijing Normal University. China Institute of Education and Social Development (CIESD) was co-founded by the China Association for Promoting Democracy and Beijing Normal University. It was founded on the basis of China Institute of Education Policy and China Academy of Social Management of Beijing Normal University. Beijing Normal University integrated the internal resources and giving solid supports to the foundation of CIESD.

Chapter 1
Investigating "Collective Individualism Learning Model": Ideas and Theories

This chapter aims to examine the diverse and complex approach in which classroom culture contributes to the shaping of students' learning cultural identity. Classroom culture plays a fundamental role in constructing students' learning competencies, perceptions, and behaviors. Thus, this study conceptualizes and contextualizes a collective individualism learning model to explicate a specific learning model in classroom culture at Chinese particular context historically and traditionally. The collective individualism model is identified as the individualized learning style of students in Chinese classroom culture characterized by nine symbolic objects including a textbook, an exercise book, a pen, a blackboard, a screen, a computer, a table, a chair, and platform in a Chinese collective class. In addition, two core components of formal collectivism and substantive individualism derived from constructive learning theory, social learning theory, Mezirow's transformative learning theory, and Kolb's experiential learning theory. The implications for examining the collective individualism model of Chinese classroom culture are likewise linked to innovative talent cultivation and fulfillment of "Four Good Teachers" goal. Both the discussion and conclusion led to the construction of promising classroom culture at the Chinese context practically.

1.1 Introduction

Students' learning outcome is deeply embedded in constructing classroom culture. Classroom culture also contributes to cultivating students' learning competencies. In China, classroom culture involves political, cultural, and economic factors. Since the 19th National Congress of the Communist Party of China, the teacher education in China has entered a new era. Both the document entitled *the Opinions on Deepening the Reform of Teachers' Construction in an All-round Way* and *the Action Plan for Revitalizing Teachers' Education and the proposition of students' core qualities* indicate that the overall educational environment for teachers' professional development

© Springer Nature Singapore Pte Ltd. 2020
X. Zhu and J. Li, *Classroom Culture in China*, Perspectives on Rethinking and Reforming Education, https://doi.org/10.1007/978-981-15-1827-0_1

has undergone tremendous changes. In the contemporary Chinese education system, teacher education is facing new challenges and the biggest challenge, which lies in how to undertake the responsibility of cultivating innovative and competitive talents within a contemporary Chinese education context. Specifically, in current China, it is pivotal to cultivate creative talents in order to accelerate Chinese economic development. Especially, the important enlightenment of the Sino-US trade war on international education lies in that the cultivation of creative talents should serve the invention of enterprise core technology and the cultivation of national spirit, which is not subject to bullying by other countries. Therefore, the mastery of core technology is considered as a powerful "weapon" of a country's competitiveness, which depends on the quality of education for the cultivation of scientific and technologically innovative talents. In this sense, the quality of education is inherently linked to one nation's comprehensive capacities and power. Through the domain of the contemporary Chinese primary education system, the merging changes in classroom culture are imbedded in shaping students' knowledge, learning skill, learning attitudes, and learning habits. Particularly, China has entered a multidimensional society, which through the major three stages of pre-modern, modern, and post-modern social development, in which parallel to agriculture, industry, and post-industry coexist. Hence, the traditional media, modern media, and Internet media are inherently intertwined with each other and put forward the demand for fair and efficient, high-quality and balanced development in order to offer high-quality education. Individual's values also contain the pluralistic orientations of tradition and modernity of the Western and Eastern culture. Especially, there is a certain gap between the subcultural values of teenagers and the values held by the adult world. As indicated above, in the current Chinese education regime, especially the current Chinese classroom cultural environment, the term collective individualism model of Chinese classroom culture is epitomized as the fundamental values that embracing the reality of the Chinese primary educational landscape. Therefore, this study is mainly divided into three major parts: the first part involves the foundations of examining the collective individualism model, which including a literature review of learning in classroom culture and learning theories relating to analyzing and constructing the collective individualism model. Moreover, a couple of theories, concentrating on shaping classroom culture is also discussed in the first part for establishing caring classroom culture; the second part focuses on ingredients of constructing collective individualism model through defining collective individualism, analyzing collective individualism, and contextualizing collective individualism; the last part concentrates on illustrating the theoretical and practical implications of implementing collective individualism model in Chinese classroom context. The conclusion on examining the collective individualism learning model in the Chinese education context is summarized to meet the goal of cultivating technological innovation in the current Chinese education system.

1.2 Foundations of Examining Collective Individualism Model of Learning

The foundations of examining the collective individualism model involve a literature review of learning in classroom culture and learning theories relating to analyzing and constructing the collective individualism model. The overview of learning in classroom culture offers a broad background to contextualize and characterize the collective individualism model. The collective individualism model is immersed in specific classroom culture in the Chinese context, which I essential to empathically response to students' thinking and reflections. In addition, the collective individualism model also integrates a couple of learning theories to epitomize Chinese classroom cultural learning with Chinese characteristics. Thus, both literature on classroom culture and learning theories contribute to examining the collective individualism model at the Chinese context.

1.2.1 Literature Review of Learning in Classroom Culture

Culture is considered as a "slippery concept" regarding the approach in which the school as an organization. Classroom culture offers various environment and atmosphere for all the stakeholders (Glover & Coleman, 2005; John & Sutherland, 2005). In addition, classroom is considered as a mixed organizational platform, including a learning environment, student–student interaction, teacher–student interaction, collaborative and group learning, selection and use of software, selection and use of other learning materials, teacher understanding of pedagogy, the impact of external pressures such as exam requirements, teacher understanding of constructed conceptual development and cognitive knowledge, the interactive learning platform as the focus for learning activity, the link between learning activities and students' interactions. Classroom culture is essential for promoting academic resiliency. The classroom environment serves as the certainty control elements. Therefore, educators are expected to consider several factors in order to construct an effective classroom cultural environment. These factors should promote students' rusting relationships with adults, building competence, confidence, and opportunities. As educators, we must continually evaluate our curriculum to find opportunities for students to engage in problem-solving and the practical application of their learning. Therefore, the responsive classroom culture might improve students' ownership of literacy learning and alleviate feeling of anger, anxiety, alienation, and powerlessness.

Theoretically, there existed a couple of theories, concentrating on shaping classroom culture. Both the constructivist psychological theories of Piaget and the radical constructivism of von Glaserfeld emphasize the interactive processes among learners within the social context of learning (Bloome, 1986; Dyson, 1992). The classroom culture is directly influencing the interactive process of learning within a social context. The roots of motivation for learning activity are deeply embedded in the sociocultural contexts of learning and the transitive processes occurring in those particular contexts. From a social constructivist perspective, the motivation for classroom learning encompasses not only the classroom culture but also includes the interpersonal and intrapersonal components for promoting students' learning process. There also existed a couple of conceptual framework to examine classroom culture, including White's effectance motivation, Weiner's Attribution theory, deCharm's (1984) theory of personal causation, Glasser's control theory, cognitive evaluation theories, and organismic integration of Deci and Ryan (1987). Overall speaking, classroom culture plays a pivotal role in students' learning satisfaction and learning achievement. If students feel comfortable in a particular classroom, they are more likely to attend or participate in the course and more willing to seek out extra assistant and more apt to cope with intellectual challenges. In other words, classroom culture is absolutely associated with student engagement and motivation in the specific learning process. Identifying a sense of belonging is considered part of the classroom community. Therefore, encouraging students to be creative and curious about the subject matter and creating a diverse classroom culture offer students' variable skills and goals serve as the fundamental task for building a particular classroom culture relatively. Moreover, classroom culture also embraces creating feelings of "student–teacher" mutual respect and connectedness, which is considered as an icebreaker activity. In this sense, classroom culture is fundamentally rooted in students' knowledge acquisition and emotional socialization. For example, Rollard (2012) argued that classroom culture involves promoting mastery, learning the content, and fostering positive student attitudes. Dweck (2000) indicated that the role of students pays much attention to create social affirmation rather than learning the content of knowledge within a particular classroom culture. However, the role of teachers more emphasized on promoting a mastery orientation through explaining the purpose of learning challenges and encouraging students to persist along with emphasizing the connections between persistence and learning. Thus, the core idea of classroom culture concentrates on stimulating students' willingness to engage with a variety of challenging tasks. In other words, there existed four major elements of classroom culture, including the ways and tasks are introduced; actions that support students in engaging with the core task; reviews of the student solutions to the task, and noncompetitive assessment processes. Rollard also suggested that classroom culture is an important determinant of the ways that students learn and the classroom culture is influenced by the actions teachers take in supporting students. Specifically, through Western classroom culture, students are expected to gain a couple of competencies, including skills of communicating and learning and individual orientation of personal needs, attention, talent, uniqueness. Practically, students may promote their various skills in particular learning pairs, groups, activities, and task within the classroom environment. Thus, classroom culture is progressively constructed through teaching–learning interaction and construction along with experience, activities, tasks, and initial creativity. To some extent, the classroom is regarded as one informal organization to build horizontal relations between teachers and students through different types of discussions and arguments. In an organizational classroom, the teacher is identified as an organizer, mentor, guide, and helper to support student-centered classroom atmosphere.

To sum up, classroom culture makes students become more motivated through choosing a positive attitude, open-mindedness, searching for worthwhileness, self-regulating attention, learning through engaging in the classroom. Establishing caring classroom culture is essential to empathically understand and response to students' thinking and reflections in order to offering classroom culture (Belenky, Clinchy, Goldberger, & Tarule, 1986; Deci & Ryan, 1990; Dewey, 1904; Erickson & Shultz, 1992). Classroom culture is also inherently associated with learning, self-esteem, and caring. The responsive classroom culture facilitated students' adaptive learning processes. The learning environment supported the motivational processes of those who were undergoing motivational struggles as well as those who were deeply engaged in literacy learning. In contrast to many studies on motivation, it was not the intent of this study to measure either motivation or achievement. We should understand and represent students' experiences as fully and fairly as possible and report it. In spite of the limitations of biased understandings of learning, Beekman (1986) suggests that positive and reactive classroom culture may deal with students' motivational struggles in order to improve the classroom literacy from a "common horizon" perspective.

1.2.2 Learning Theories' Perspective on Epitomizing Collective Individualism Model

Overall speaking, the collective individualism model integrates a couple of learning theories to epitomize Chinese classroom cultural learning with Chinese characteristics. Both formal collectivism and substantive individualism serve as core components to construct the collective individualism model with Chinese characteristics. Specifically, in the collective individualism learning model, the core component of substantive individualism of the collective individualism model derived from constructive learning theory. The core component of formal collectivism in the collective individualism model is inherently rooted in social learning theory. The interactions of "peer to peer" and "student to teacher" are fundamentally epitomized through both Mezirow's transformative learning theory and Kolb's experiential learning theory.

1.2.3 A Constructive Learning Theory Perspective on Collective Individualism Model

In the collective individualism learning model, the core component of substantive individualism in the collective individualism model derived from constructive learning theory. Specifically, the constructive learning theory highlighted that the pedagogy effectively supports students' learning and the effective pedagogy should be responsive to students' instructional experiences. Specifically, the idea of constructivism is originated from Piaget's pedagogy, involving two basic principles. These two principles include: one is knowledge is not passively received but actively built up by the cognizing subject; another is the function of cognition is adaptive and serves to organize the experiential world, not to discover an ontological reality. The core idea of constructivism is that new knowledge is mainly constructed from previous knowledge. In other words, learning is a constructive process through understanding and interacting with experiences. Knowledge is associated with individuals' cognitive activity, including the particular process of observations, interpreting outcomes, making predictions, and solving problems. The consistency of knowing, learning, and experiencing is immersed in individual constructive cognition. The thinking and reasoning process is interacted in the process of knowing, learning, and experiencing.

Along with the prior illustration of constructive learning theory, the collective individualism learning model follows the core ideas that divide knowledge into procedural knowledge, which focuses on offering an instrumental understanding of the content. Within the collective individualism classroom, students possess the procedural and conceptual understanding of knowledge. In this sense, students create new knowledge by bridging new ideas to existing ones with a robust and durable understanding of knowledge. In other words, within the collective individualism learning model, the core features of substantive individualism examine how students learn instead of a teaching method. Thus, the idea of substantive individualism is parallel to constructivist teaching and constructivist pedagogy. Practically, in order to improve the efficiency of learning at the classroom of collective individualism, instructional learning strategy is advocated to foster an understanding of teaching. In this sense, students' thinking should be of key interest to the teacher, not their behavior. When teaching an idea, the teacher must elicit students' thinking and listen closely in order to form an adequate model of the students' current ways of thinking about that idea so that he or she can determine the means to further develop it.

1.2.4 Social Cultural Learning Theory Perspective on Collective Individualism Model

In the collective individualism learning model, the core component of formal collectivism of the collective individualism model is inherently rooted in social learning theory. Social learning theory refers to one type of learning behaviors, constructing through observing and imitating peers. The learning process is considered as a cognitive process that existed in a different social context. The social learning also involves the observation of rewards, punishments, and reinforcement. This theory expands on traditional behavioral theories, in which behavior is governed solely by reinforcements, by placing emphasis on the important roles of various internal processes in the learning individual. In this sense, the core component of formal collectivism of the collective individualism model combined both behavioral and cognitive learning theories to offer a comprehensive learning model. Within the collective individualism classroom, learning is not purely behavioral, and it is a cognitive process that takes place in a social context. The student learning process occurs by observing a behavior and by observing the consequences of the behavior or vicarious reinforcement. Formal collectivism as one core component involves observation, extraction of information from those observations, and making decisions about the performance of the behavior and observational learning or modeling. Thus, the formal collective learning could occur without an observable change in behavior. Reinforcement plays a role in learning but is not entirely responsible for learning. In a collective individualism classroom, the learner is not a passive recipient of the information and the cognition, environment, and behavior all mutually influence each other.

Transformative learning theory on collective individualism model
In collective individualism learning model, the interactions of student–student and student–teacher is fundamentally epitomized through both Mezirow's transformative learning theory and Kolb's experiential learning theory. Specifically, Mezirow's transformative learning theory highlights the significance of recursive learning experience and learning process in order to facilitate the collective individualism learning model. Moreover, Mezirow's (2000) transformative theory emphasizes several steps of recursive process, including experiencing a disorienting dilemma, experiencing fear, anger, guilt, or shame, critically assessing assumptions about the world, realizing others have gone through what they are feeling, revising one's old belief system and exploring new ones, planning a course of action, gaining the knowledge and skills for implementing new plans, trying on the new role, becoming competent and confident with the new change and reintegrating into one's life based on a new perspective.

Additionally, within collective individualism classroom, students' learning experience is gained through "peer to peer" connection and "teacher to student" interaction. Along with Dewey, Kolb's experiential learning theory highlights the importance of learning experience in the learning process. In a collective individualism classroom, the concrete experience asks individuals to engage in a learning context and abstract conceptualization focuses on logical thinking and rational evaluation to integrate observation into logical theories. Reflective observation involves tentative and impartial dimensions towards the learning process. Active experimentation concentrates on examining previously generated ideas. In other words, in Kolb's learning model, flexibility of "peer to peer" connection and "teacher to student" interaction is considered as a key factor to offer an effective approach. More importantly, the proposed collective individualism model follows and synthesizes the historical development of learning theories. For instance, in the historical development of learning theories, Bloom's taxonomy involves higher-order thinking skills, focusing on analyzing, synthesizing, and evaluating. John Dewey (1933) furthermore examined the issues of learning problems and challenges. Since the 1960s, the proliferation of learning theories has produced numerous social scientists in education. In particular, Rogers proposed client-centered therapy and student-centered education in accordance with personal involvement, self-initiation, pervasiveness, evaluation by the learner, its essence is meaning. Without a doubt, Rogers argued that teachers serve as facilitators at the "learner self-evaluation" movement. Moreover, Gagne (1972) suggested that the effective learning theory includes five domains of the learning process, such as motor skills, verbal information, intellectual skills, cognitive strategies, and attitudes, which are learned most effectively through the use of human models and "vicarious reinforcement". Consisting of the study of Gagne, Gardner (1983) proposed the theory of multiple intelligences theory, including different kinds of intelligence. Hence, we found that each emerging learning model or theory inherits prior fundamental and classical learning theories, such as Thorndike's Connectionism, Pavlov's Classical Conditioning, Guthrie's Contiguous Conditioning, Skinner's Operant Conditioning, Hull's Systematic Behavior Theory, Tolman's Purposive Behaviorism, Gestalt Theory, Freud's Psychodynamics, Functionalism, Mathematical Learning Theory, and Information Processing Models. With no doubt, the proposed collective individualism model definitely serves as the "inherited product" of the learning model.

In conclusion, along with the analysis of constructive learning theory, social learning theory, transformative learning theory, and experiential learning theory, the core learning components of collective individualism learning model are divided into procedural knowledge, instrumental knowledge, observing and imitating learning, interaction of "peer to peer" and "teacher to student". As the illustration previously, constructive learning theory, social learning theory, transformative learning theory, and experiential learning theory all contribute to offering a solid foundation to explore the learning logic and learning process of the collective individualism learning model

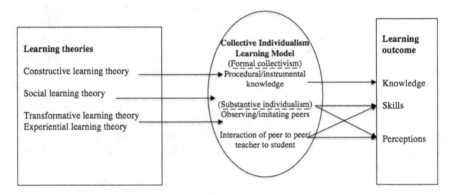

Fig. 1.1 Process pathway of the collective individualism learning model

in the Chinese context. In addition, the core components of procedural knowledge, instrumental knowledge, observing and imitating learning, interaction of "peer to peer" and "teacher to student" are interdependent with each other. The learning outcome involves knowledge, skills, and attitudes, which is consistent with the collective individualism model. Thus, the collective individualism model is linked between learning theories and learning outcomes (see Fig. 1.1).

1.3 Constructing Collective Individualism Learning Model

The proposed collective individual model is epitomized through defining collective individualism, analyzing collective individualism, and contextualizing collective individualism. Specifically, defining collective individualism involves examining a particular concept and context within classroom culture in Chinese particular education system. Analyzing collective individualism focuses on investigating Chinese traditional pedagogy by illustrating the teacher–student relation with Chinese characteristics, which is characterized as the collective individual relation. Contextualizing collective individualism focuses on the integration of the collective individual model of classroom culture and the process of cultivating innovative talents in the contemporary education system. Thus, the term collective individual model of Chinese classroom culture systematically combined historical, political, and social elements into constructing classroom culture with Chinese characteristics.

Defining collective individualism

The term collective individual model is mainly associated with a particular concept and context within classroom culture in Chinese particular education system. The term collective individualism model refers to the individualized learning style of the students in Chinese classroom culture characterized by nine symbolic objects, including a textbook, an exercise book, a pen, a blackboard, a screen, a computer, a table, a chair, and a platform in a Chinese collective class. It has the characteristics of collectivity in form and individuality in essence. All those nine symbolic objects represent the core expression of identifying collective individualism classroom culture. In other words, the so-called "Nine Symbolic Objects" embrace both formal collectivism and substantive individual characteristics in Chinese-characterized classroom culture. Specifically, "the formal collectivism" require students must obey the classroom principles and orders with the restriction of objective educational resources, such as the symbolic materials of the textbook, exercise book, pen, blackboard, screen, computer, table, chair, and platform. Meanwhile, "substantive individual" reveals that student as an independent learner has the tendency to create different specific learning methods and offer various learning habits. In this sense, within the Chinese classroom, the term collective individual model unveils the "intra-extra learning communication" pedagogy with Chinese characteristics. Specifically, the "intra learning" reflects students serve as independent learner, who holds specific individual recognition and experiences. Comparing with intra-learning, the extra

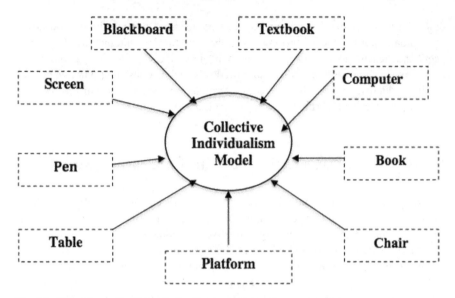

Fig. 1.2 "Nine Symbolic Objects" of collective individualism model of classroom culture

learning require student as one part of the collective group and must obey the required classroom regulars and conditions. Hence, the "intra-extra learning communication" pedagogy is fundamentally intertwined in identifying the collective individual model (see Fig. 1.2).

Analyzing collective individualism learning model
The collective individual model of Chinese contextual classroom culture is deeply embedded in traditional Chinese pedagogy. In traditional Chinese pedagogical regime, student–teacher relation in the Chinese context is identified as a teacher-dominated learning model through classroom culture. Comparing with Western class-room culture, Eastern classroom culture mainly involves gaining knowledge from teachers, textbooks, and collective consciousness. In the context of Chinese class-room, learning is considered as a performance, encompassing a variety of presenta-tion, repetition, and memorization. The relationship between teacher and students is parallel to the listener and reader in a specific contextualized communication flow. Hierarchical relations reflect a mode of agreement, harmony, and respect. In other words, in traditional Chinese pedagogy, the teacher serves as a model and expert with absolute authority in accordance with Chinese teacher-centered classroom culture. This specific contextualized teacher-centered classroom culture is the combination ideology of Buddhism, Taoism, and Confucianism, which offers the underpinnings of Chinese inhabitable pedagogies and cultural expression. Historically, the "almond altar" (Confucius's lecture place) is regarded as the Chinese earliest symbolic class-room. It is a legend that Confucius was sitting on the altar and giving lectures to his disciples. The almond altar is characterized to epitomize the nature of collective individualism. The teaching and learning interactive mode between Confucius and

his disciples also reflects the essential nature of the collective individual relations. In addition, in ancient China, private school refers to home school with a private tutor, which was a kind of folk preschool education institution in the ancient Chinese education system. It is a private school run by a knowledgeable master in order to disseminate Confucianism. The informal private school is also considered a vivid symbolic example to describe the historical origin of traditional Chinese classroom culture. The teacher taught a series of textbooks, focusing on *Confucian Classics, such as Analects of Confucius, University, Doctrine of the Mean, Meng Zi, Book of Rites* and *Book of Changes.* In conclusion, both almond altar and ancient Chinese private schools contribute to refining and constructing the collective individual model of contextual Chinese classroom culture. Along with ancient Chinese classroom culture, the teacher–student relation with Chinese characteristics is profoundly characterized as the collective individual relation. Within the classroom, teacher–student relation refers to the mutual relationship between teachers and students in the process of teaching and learning, including their position, role, and attitude towards each other. It is also a special social and interpersonal relationship contextually. By this logic, it is also a multi-nature and multilevel relation system formed by teachers and students through direct communication activities between teaching and learning in their respective unique identities and positions. The embodiment of pedagogical value and meaning reveals in specific teaching and learning activities. Moreover, in accordance with traditional Chinese pedagogical idea regarding "*respecting teachers and emphasizing education*", teachers have always been in a highly respected position in the strict class and social hierarchy of ancient China. Because of the scarcity of educational resources, teachers are in an absolutely dominant position in the process of education. In Chinese pedagogical tradition of "*respecting teachers and emphasizing education*", ancient Chinese teachers should insist on the responsibility of "*one day as a teacher, a lifetime as a father.*" In this sense, the relationship between teachers and students is not only a teacher–student relationship, but also a father–son relationship. Therefore, the teacher also has a kind of "family care" for their students. Chinese teachers often called their students as "disciples" to express their love for their students. In addition, from the feudal etiquette perspective, ancient China raised the status of teachers to an absolute position, giving the emperor the same political treatment to guarantee teachers playing a dominated role within teaching–learning interaction. In this sense, from a historical perspective, the collective individual model of classroom culture vividly unveils the teacher–student relation with Chinese characteristics.

Contextualizing collective individualism learning model
In contemporary Chinese education system, how to integrate the collective individual model of classroom culture into the process of cultivating innovative talents is considered the key mission for the Chinese central government. Balancing the collectivism and individualism is pivotal to reconstruct the collective individual model of Chinese classroom culture in order to cultivate innovative talents for accelerating Chinese economic and technology development. In recent years, the Chinese central government gradually paid much attention to improving classroom culture in order to

cultivate innovative talents. For example, President Xi Jinping initially proposed the goal of "*Four Good Teachers*", identifying a Chinese good teacher should have ideals and beliefs, moral sentiment, solid knowledge, and benevolence. The goal of "*Four Good Teachers*" is initiated on the eve of the 30th Chinese Teacher's Day in 2014 and President Xi Jinping encouraged the teachers and students to be the example of "*Fourth Good Teachers*" during his visit to Beijing Normal University. This political goal of "*Fourth Good Teachers*" provided the important direction that Chinese teachers must cultivate and undertake in the process of integration and penetration of education in order to improve Chinese students' innovative competencies. Along with implementing the national goal of "*Fourth Good Teachers*", Chinese teachers encountered tremendous challenges and barriers to integrate Chinese inhabitable classroom culture into current education requirements. Moreover, with Chinese traditional cultural heritage, the collective individualism model of classroom culture is vulnerable to examine the real landscape of student–teacher relations among contextualized classroom culture. There is a tendency for Chinese teachers to reconstruct teacher–students relations in order to cultivate innovative talents. Moreover, in accordance with the rapid development of Chinese education, Chinese classroom culture is expected to be regarded as open, dynamic systems influenced by the espoused values of the society being served and resulting from multiple interpretations, interactions, and negotiations of individuals and groups (Schoen & Teddlie, 2008). The classroom is considered as space where containing cultural traditions within a society or where existing and unjust cultural, political, and economic structures are critically addressed, challenged, and transformed (Schoen & Teddlie, 2008). Nevertheless, the nature of teacher–student activities is essential to shape classroom culture. Liu (2006) argued that classroom culture is connected to school effectiveness and school reform for creating the dynamics of interaction between schools and communities. Although different classrooms may have its own particular culture, there is a general dynamic process of learning in every school (Liu, 2006).

Socialization is also inherently embedded in Chinese classroom culture and aims to construct more social activities (Renold, 2006). Classroom culture actively produces student–teacher-dominant relations in the society of the hegemonic process (Dobbs, Arnold, & Doctoroff, 2004; Robinson & Jones Diaz, 2006). Classroom culture is also intertwined with school organization and management structures, teachers' attitude, expectations, and interactions with the teaching language, the curriculum, disciplinary approaches, and students' own characteristics (Connell, 2006; Liu, 2006; Robinson & Jones Diaz, 2006). In addition, the classroom culture of the school defines gendered behavior for its inhabitants, teachers and students play a key role in the way in which femininities and masculinities are mediated and lived out through actively negotiating and reproducing gender identities for themselves and others (Liu, 2006; Mac an Ghaill, 1994). Hence, to some extent, classroom culture is identified to be successful to embrace the hegemonic socialization process. In conclusion, the emerging collective individual model embraces "defining-analyzing-contextualizing" stages to summarize classroom culture with Chinese characteristics. Comparing with modern Western classroom culture, Chinese classroom culture more likely to obey traditional Chinese pedagogy and respect teachers' absolute authority.

In other words, the contemporary classroom culture with Chinese characteristics is parallel to combining pedagogical ideas of Confucianism, which offers the underpinnings of Chinese traditional culture. Hence, as the illustration above, the teacher–student relation with Chinese characteristics is characterized as the collective individual relation. In reality, in accordance with the national goal of "Fourth Good Teachers", the Chinese government encountered tremendous challenges and barriers to combine Chinese-characterized classroom culture into current education requirements. Moreover, with traditional Chinese cultural heritage, the collective individualism model of classroom culture is subject to explore the student–teacher relations among contextualized classroom culture. Moreover, the process of socialization is also associated with Chinese classroom culture in order to cultivate students' social perceptions, behaviors, and habits.

1.4 Discussion, Implication, and Conclusion

In the era of rapid accelerating information and technology, China, like all other countries in the world, is on the road to the development of artificial intelligence. Chinese society has entered an era of coexistence of natural intelligence and artificial intelligence. It poses challenges to Chinese contemporary education at different levels. In order to cultivate innovative talents, we should not only cultivate their ability to master artificial intelligence, but also teach them to coexist with artificial intelligence. From the teachers' perspective, they should not only apply artificial intelligence for their teaching but also compete with artificial intelligence for their learning. In the educational environment, especially within classrooms, the collective individualism model of classroom culture is inherently imbedded in traditional Chinese pedagogical paradigm of cultivating Chinese talents. In the contemporary Chinese education system, along with the globalization and internationalization forces in different countries' educational regime, China's education has a tendency to enter a "learner-centered" era and teachers are more likely to be a supplement role to support students to gain a variety of knowledge and skills. In recent decades, in accordance with neoliberalism, more and more private international schools at the mainland of China advocated the idea of "student-centered" teacher–student relations through choosing a positive attitude, open-mindedness, searching for worthwhileness, self-regulating attention, learning through engaging in the classroom. Moreover, "*Fourth Good Teachers*" has shown that Chinese today's society offers a couple of expectations and requirements. Thus, current Chinese teachers have to face the indisputable challenges and barriers brought about by complex social transitions. In reality, the relation between Chinese teachers and students is synthesized in the model of collective individualism classroom culture. Hence, how to find a pathway to integrate and balance "student-centered" and "teacher-centered" classroom culture to cultivate creative talents comprehensively? Thus, it is inevitable to adjust or reform the current existing collective individualism model of the Chinese classroom. Creating and providing a more friendly classroom culture for shaping teacher–student relation aims to develop teachers' professional consciousness and cultivate creative Chinese talents. In other words, the promising classroom culture is subject to offer students learning imagination, learning curiosity, multi-thinking, problem-solving competencies for promoting students' comprehensive creativity. In other words, the promising classroom culture should stimulate students to observe, discover, think, debate, experience, and comprehend in the process of learning. It is a real classroom culture in which students gradually master the skills and knowledge of discovering, raising, thinking, finding information, and drawing conclusions. More importantly, it is also facing major scientific and technological challenges to create a good social atmosphere and to achieve the coordinated developmental relations of "human and nature", "human and human", "human and society". The promising classroom culture also should be in consistent with the need of cultivating students' emotional skills to cultivate specific classroom culture. It should also focus on shaping the classroom culture that provides students with the independent spirit to learn and acquire aesthetic and artistic awareness and competencies. Overall speaking, we need to adjust current Chinese classroom culture in order to shape a promising classroom culture full of knowledge, technology, and spiritual content, which can play a role in the purpose and means at the same time. The formation of a new classroom culture obviously requires teachers to possess the ability to construct classroom culture. The ability to construct classroom culture is the ability to construct the knowledge framework for student's development goals and learning, but also the ability to promote students' cognitive and emotional development, moral and civic development, personality and social development, healthy and safe development, art and aesthetic development. In addition, teachers should construct the system and spiritual classroom culture for students' comprehensive development and should construct classroom culture based on students' learning attributes and features. In this sense, deconstructing the current collective individualism model of classroom culture is beneficial to the cultivation of creative talents.

To sum up, practically, along with the elaboration previously, for Chinese teachers, there are the following points need to be highlighted: first, reducing the number of students in the class, expanding and enriching classroom learning resources are essential for Chinese teachers to create professional learning classroom culture for students; second, reducing the proportion of knowledge and memory, improving working memory and physical memory is the key to stimulate students' learning motivation and passion. Integrating the current achievements of brain science and cognitive science into the process of teaching and learning is fundamental to promote students' comprehensive growth; third, reducing the amount of individualistic learning tasks and increase the proportion of cooperating learning tasks also provide an effective approach to enhance students' cooperation awareness and competencies. Moreover, Chinese teachers should build the cognitive training goal of maintaining attention and memory and expanding the proportion of project learning in problem-solving cognitive ability, which is the inevitable requirement for teachers to cultivate creative talents. Only in this way can Chinese teachers really achieve the expectation goal of "*Four good Teachers*".

References

Allard, A., & Cooper, M. (2001). 'Learning to cooperate': A study of how primary teachers and children construct classroom cultures. *Asia-Pacific Journal of Teacher Education, 29*(2), 153–169. https://doi.org/10.1080/13598660120061336.

Beekman, T. (1986). Stepping inside: On participant experience and bodily presence in thefield. *Journal of Education, 168*(3), 43.

Belenky, M., Clinchy, B., Goldberger, N., & Tarule, J. (1986). *Women's ways of knowing: The development of self, voice and mind.* NewYork: Basic Books.

Bloome, D. (1986). Reading as a social process in a middle school classroom. In D. Bloome (Ed.), *Literacy and schooling* (pp. 123–149). Norwood, NJ: Ablex.

Connell, R. W. (2006). Understanding men: Gender sociology and the new international research on masculinities. In C. Skelton, B. Francis, & L. Smulyan (Eds.), *The SAGE handbook of gender and education* (pp. 18–30). London: Sage.

deCharms, R. (1984). Motivation enhancement in educational settings. In R. E. Ames & C. Ames (Eds.), *Research on motivation on education: Vol. 1. Student motivation* (pp. 275–312). New York: Academic Press.

Deci, E. L., & Ryan, R. M. (1987). *Intrinsic motivation and self-determination in human behavior.* New York: Plenum.

Deci, E., & Ryan, R. (1990). *A motivational approach to self: Integration in personality.* Paper presented to the Nebraska symposium on motivation, Lincoln, NE.

Dewey, J. (1904). The relation of theory to practice in education. In C. A. McMurry (Ed.), *Third yearbook, Part I. National society for the scientific study of education* (pp. 9–30). Chicago: University of Chicago Press.

Dewey, J. (1933). *How we think: A restatement of the relation of reflective thinking to the educative process.* New York, NY: D. C. Health and Co.

Dobbs, J., Arnold, D. H., & Doctoroff, G. L. (2004). Attention in the preschool classroom: The relationships among child gender, child misbehavior, and types of teacher attention. *Early Child Development and Care, 174*(3), 281–295.

Dweck, C. S. (1975). The role of expectations and attributions in the alleviation of learned helplessness. *Journal of Personality and Social Psychology, 31*(4), 674–685.

Dweck, C. S. (2000). *Self-theories: Their role in motivation, personality, and development.* Philadelphia: Psychology Press.

Dyson, A. H. (1992). Whistle for Willie, lost puppies, and cartoon dogs: The sociocultural dimensions of young children's composing. *Journal of Reading Behavior, 24*(4), 433–462.

Erickson, F., & Shultz, J. (1992). Students' experience of the curriculum. In P. W. Jackson (Ed.), *Handbook of research on curriculum* (pp. 465–485). New York: Macmillan.

Gagne, R. M. (1972). Domains of learning. *Interchange,* 1–8.

Gardner, H. (1983). *Frames of mind: The theory of multiple intelligences.* New York, NY: Basic Books.

Glover, D., & Coleman, M. (2005). School climate, culture and ethos: interchangeable or distinctive concepts? *Journal of In-service Education, 31*(2), 251–272.

John, P., & Sutherland, R. (2005). Affordance, opportunity and pedagogical implications of ICT. *Educational Review, 57*(4), 405–413.

Liu, F. (2006). School culture and gender. In C. Skelton, B. Francis, & L. Smulyan (Eds.), *The SAGE handbook of gender and education* (pp. 425–438). London: Sage.

Mac an Ghaill, M. (1994). The making of men: Masculinities, sexualities, and schooling. Buckingham: Open University Press.

Mezirow, J. (2000). Learning to think like an adult: Transformation theory: Core concepts. In J. Mezirow & Associates (Eds.), *Learning as trans-formation: Critical perspectives on a theory in progress* (pp. 3–33). San Francisco: Jossey-Bass.

Renold, E. (2006). Gendered classroom experiences. In C. Skelton, B. Francis, & L. Smulyan (Eds.), *The SAGE handbook of gender and education* (pp. 439–452). London: Sage.

Robinson, K. H., & Jones Diaz, C. (2006). *Diversity and difference in early childhood education: Issues for theory and practice.* Berkshire: Open University Press.

Rollard, R. G. (2012). Synthesizing the evidence on classroom goal structures in middle and secondary schools: A meta analysis and narrative review. *Review of Educational Research, 82*(4), 396–435.

Schoen, L., & Teddlie, C. (2008). A new model of school culture: A response to a call for conceptual clarity. *School Effectiveness and School Improvement, 19*(2), 129–153.

Chapter 2
Contextualizing "Collective Individualism Learning": A Chinese Classroom Cultural Perspective

This chapter concentrates on contextualizing "Collective Individualism Learning" from the perspective of the Chinese model of classroom culture. It involves the introduction of classroom learning with Chinese characteristics, the material and cultural characteristics of "nine one" classrooms of collective individual learning, the connotative construction of collective individual learning, and the conclusion related to constructing collective individual learning model.

2.1 Introduction on Classroom Learning with Chinese Characteristics

There existed a couple of studies on Chinese classroom learning for a long time, mostly put forward by Western scholars, based on the learning theory of Western learning theory based on the main scientific positivism and based on methods such as logical positivism, but we found that the lack of learning theory on middle school students to learn specific classroom culture, such that Thorndike's learning is through trial and error and form a bond between stimulus and response, bandura think learning is acquired by observing the behavior of imitation role-models new behavior and the learning is the understanding of symbolic meaning and form the cognitive map, they don't have a classroom culture of narrative logic. Although their narrative view has prevalent meaning for "migration" of learning in the classroom culture, such as can Thorndike narrative that deduces for students to learn in the classroom through trial and error and form a bond between stimulus and response, can also keep the bandura narrative expression for students in the classroom culture learning by observing the behavior of imitation as fugleman of teacher and students and learned behavior, it also can put the narrative understanding for students to learn through understanding of the significance of symbols in the classroom to form a cognitive map, but the narrative doesn't reveal the classroom, especially Chinese common student learning in the classroom culture of common mode. This general pattern is the

© Springer Nature Singapore Pte Ltd. 2020
X. Zhu and J. Li, *Classroom Culture in China*, Perspectives on Rethinking and Reforming Education, https://doi.org/10.1007/978-981-15-1827-0_2

"collective individual learning pattern" discussed in this paper, which is unique to China's classroom culture. What is the unique classroom culture in China? What is collective individual learning? What are the characteristics of collective individual learning in China's unique classroom environment? Before answering these questions, it is important to explain why the author of this article is concerned about them. Foreign education professional experts after graduation engaged in comparative education research, from the beginning only focus on foreign education, or a nation-state and the macroscopic research of education development, to visit into classroom microscopic study of the country, gradually formed the two basic problems, a problem compared with the education of different countries in the world, the uniqueness of Chinese education performance in where? Another question is how do different educations produce creative people? Related to the two issues, the international large-scale PISA rankings show Chinese students doing well in mathematics, but not in creativity, reading, and science. This prompts us to ask why students do well in math in China's unique classroom culture. As the same time, it also inspired us to focus on the study of classroom culture, especially the research related to the classroom cultural environment, this experience focuses on the classroom culture and students learning to construct logical relationship and there is a kind of theoretical innovation one might expect, this kind of looking forward to this article is to discuss the Chinese middle school students learning in the classroom "collective individual learning mode." Through reading the literature, the concept similar to "collective individual" should be "collective individualism", which is "a phenomenon in which a single group makes value and behavior choices only based on its own interests." The internal logic of this concept is "acting on the individual through the collective," which exists in an intermediary form. But the concept of collective individual learning is abstracted from Chinese classroom culture.[1]

2.2   Material and Cultural Characteristics of "Nine One" Classrooms of Collective Individual Learning

Collective individual learning exists in the material culture of Chinese classrooms characterized by "nine ones". We call it the material cultural foundation of collective individual learning in classrooms. The question is what is "nine one" classroom material culture? The so-called "nine" classroom material culture refers to a book, a pen, and a workbook or personal have characterized the homework, a podium, a blackboard, a screen, a computer for public performance and characteristics of the characteristics of a table, a chair for unity in the classroom of physical space. Obviously, "nine one" classroom material culture has the characteristics of private, public, unity, and authority.

---

[1] Li Juntang. Towards meaningful division of labor: construction of real collective education in schools. Science of Education, 2014 (6):23–27.

1. Personal characteristics. Personal, this classroom culture, refers to the students in the learning process that individuals have a book, a pen, and a workbook or the state of exercise books, each student may seem fair to have a book, a pen, and a book, they are "holy" aggression, which directly determines the respective individual students to take their individualism characteristics of learning in the classroom.

2. Public features. It emphasizes the commonality of classroom culture, which highlighting the core value of global shared community. The core public features of classroom culture is to provide the collective learning in the classroom. The material culture of "nine one" classrooms shows private and public characteristics similar to the difference between private goods and public goods. The nature of these two classroom cultures is closely related to the learning process of students in the classroom.

3. Unity features. In the classroom culture, this feature shows the uniform arrangement and "uniformity" of a table and a chair in the classroom. It provides the same use opportunities for each student, and their uniformity provides an undifferentiated learning mode for each student to move around the classroom.

4. Authoritative features. It is widespread in the traditional Chinese classroom culture with the characteristics of publicity. In the traditional context, teachers with the authoritative status have common teaching material to interpret different kinds of knowledge without considering the specification of classroom environment.[2]

2.3 The Connotative Construction of Collective Individual Learning

The discussion of the classroom cultural characteristics of collective individual learning lays the foundation for constructing the connotation of collective individual learning. The first concept to be understood in collective individual learning is "learning". What is learning? As mentioned in the "problem raising" of this paper, learning theorists' understanding of the concept of learning is the meaning of "learning" in the theory of learning. "Learning" in the theory of learning refers to all acquired experience, in which all the animal regulating activities of the body, such as classical conditioning and operant conditioning, are included. "Learning" in pedagogy is supported by thinking, a process in which people acquire experience through thinking processing under the action of external things. It is narrower in meaning than the concept of "learning" in the theory of learning. Obviously, collective individual learning discussed in this paper is a process in which students acquire experience through thinking under the action of "nine one" external things in the classroom environment, and it is not a complete connotation of the concept of "learning" in the theory of learning.

---

[2]Translated by Samuel bowles and Herbert kindles. Cooperative species—reciprocity and evolution of humans [M]. Hangzhou: Zhejiang University Press, 2015:3.

According to the etymology of the concept of learning and the core connotation embodied in the theoretical interpretation, we define collective individual learning as a process of lasting and stable changes of individual cognition, behavior, ability, and tendency caused by students' observation of imitation, practice, or training in the collective classroom environment with the help of teachers' and students' language and experience. The experience here includes life experience and indirect experience. "Learning refers to the more lasting changes in the behavior, ability and psychological tendency of learners caused by experience. These changes are not caused by maturity, disease, or drugs, and do not necessarily manifest outward behavior." Collective individual learning has the characteristics of social anthropology. It is not only the process of individual socialization, but also the interactive process of collective and classroom environment, as well as the active participation of individuals in the construction of collective community, but also the process of individuals shaping and changing themselves in the community. From this point of view, the concept of collective individual learning is related to the personality and social development of students. In our dimensional construction of student development, individuality and sociality are important dimensions. The development of students has both personality development and social development, and personality development and social development are the correspondence between the two aspects of the existence of "personality" and "sociality".[3]

Collective individual learning has the characteristics of information philosophy. It is the process of obtaining information through observation and imitation with the help of collective language and experience, and also the process of acquiring collective and individual consciousness, experience and knowledge in the cognition and practice of learners. The collective individual learning based on the brain is the "holistic meaning construction learning, which comprehensively reflects the holistic learning view, social learning view and situational learning view, and reflects the constructiveness and situational infiltration of collective individual learning. The collective individual learning of environmental action theory refers to the collective individual learning of students in the classroom cultural environment and psychological environment. Here the change of body and mind means the development of a person."

2.4 Collective Individual Learning Model

Collective individual learning model is composed of many concepts, including collective and collective learning, individualism and individual learning, collective individual and its learning, learning model, and so on.

Collectivity. Similar concepts with collectivity include group, social, group, team, community, etc. In school, collectivity is manifested in class, etc. The concept of

---

[3]Misaki Sato. Trans. Yu Lili. Educational methodology [M]. Beijing: Educational Science Press, 2016:82.

collective will involve the concept of collective behavior. The collective behavior of students in the classroom culture we discuss is different from the social behavior discussed in sociology but based on the behavioral characteristics of the class. In education organized by schools, the collective is a hierarchical concept, which is composed of school collective, grade collective, class collective and group collective. For students, this kind of collective is specifically programmed, that is, students are systematically arranged from a family group with a blood relationship to a hierarchical collective, which obviously has mandatory characteristics naturally. Students are "forcibly placed into a hierarchical collective without self-will." The question of what is learning, like all other questions, has the characteristics of uncertainty, with numerous views, but no matter how different the views are, there are always some key elements in common. The key elements in the definition of learning include learners and experience.[4]

Group learning. When a teacher gives classroom instruction, in most cases, students' learning is collective and concerted, and they even complete individual learning tasks within the specified time. Of course, group discussion is also adopted, but it is manifested in the process rather than result-oriented cooperation. Sometimes teachers will blame a student for not learning according to the collective requirements, which shows the disadvantages of collective individual learning models and inhibits the free choice of students' individualism. The same behavior under the same command does not mean collective, such as boarding a train. Group discussion is group behavior and does not mean inevitable collectivity. Only group behavior guided by goals and directed to results can be called collective. The same behavior under the same command does not mean collectivity, but from the perspective of school management, when the school evaluates a teacher, it ranks the teacher in the name of the class, which has the characteristics of target-led and result-oriented. Collective learning is the process of students' collective learning consciousness, emotion, and action. Collective learning consciousness is students' cognition, emotional internalization, and representation of the United State of learning. Collective learning can control, export emotional care, and arouse common memory through learning habits, so as to shape students' collective learning consciousness. Collective learning consciousness also continuously shapes and regulates students' learning behavior and their relationship with classmates, promoting a more community learning collective. For students, from a non-consanguinity, even without geographical identity, through the formation of collective learning consciousness, gradually formed a mature human relationship.

Personal learning. Similar to the individual character, the concept of individual, advocating personalized in education, for student's individuality development choice of content, way and method, and to evaluate its, therefore puts forward the concept of personalized learning, shows that the concept should fully respect the students' subjectivity, should reflect students' self-esteem and self-confidence, to create experimental hands-on opportunities for students, for students to set up extensive and varied and contact the actual course of life, and, more importantly, for students to

---

[4]Yuan Yuan. Human nature and social order [M]. Beijing: Huaxia Publishing House, 2015:33.

create learning space except "nine" and the environment. However, personal learning as understood in this paper is based on students' personal characteristics of "nine one" classrooms under the premise of collective learning, including content, methods, methods, and evaluation. This kind of individual learning and school, classroom, etc., are a heterogeneous group is related to the heterogeneity of the collective, of course, is made up of individual extremely distinct features, although can be shaped by the cultivation of the consciousness of collective learning in the collective learning emotion, relation between the individual and the collective heterogeneity determines the learning characteristics of the individual. From the perspective of individualism, there will be two views, one is possessive and egoistic individualism, and the other is ethical and altruistic individualism. They also show both in the learning process, especially in collective individual learning.[5]

Collective individual learning model. Based on the construction two concepts of collective learning and individual learning, we explain the concept of collective personal learning mode for in a fixed time and space, often in the classroom for the space and form by the stipulated time, the students sitting in a chair of unity and the table in the form of collective individuality by holding a book, a pen, and a workbook, around the public a blackboard, a podium, a computer, a screen, led by teachers of learning and learning styles. Chinese school classroom learning is mainly based on collective individual learning performance, students perform in the form of collective learning behavior or way of the human body, students holding a book, a pen, a workbook sat at his desk and chair individualized to listening to the teacher or teachers and students constitute a one-to-one or collective dialogue. The learning process of collective individual learning has the characteristics of collective in form and individualism in essence, which is decided by a textbook, a pen, and an exercise book. In collective individualistic learning, the individuality of the learning process and the individuality of the learning results are unified. In the collective individual learning model, the communication model between teachers and students is a collective communication model, and students express their own views in the collective individual learning model has certain reservations and certainty.

The collective personal learning model includes two types of cooperative learning groups: one is a process of cooperative learning group and another is a result of the combination of cooperation learning group. This is related to our learning result needs. If it is reflected by "individual achievement", then it is mainly evaluated by individualism. If it is expressed by "collective achievement" or "group achievement", it will be evaluated by combining the collectivity of process and the individuality of result. If we understand the cooperative learning of middle school students in class according to the anthropological principle that "cooperation refers to people engaging in mutually beneficial activities with others", then the collectivity in collective individual learning has the characteristics of mutual benefit. The question is how to achieve mutual benefit. Because the mutual benefit is manifested in common pursuit, full cooperation, transaction, common maintenance, etc., what is a common pursuit

---

[5]Introduction to learning theory [M]. Shanghai: Shanghai Education Press, 2011:12.

in learning? Working together what? Trade what? Joint maintenance of what? Collective individual learning model refers to a learning organization state in the classroom culture characterized by "nine ones". The external form of this learning organization state shows the collective characteristics, that is, all learners with unified desks and chairs as the basic conditions toward the blackboard and teachers to form a listening and interactive learning model. In the collective individual learning model, the "seminar" organized by teachers in class is the collective learning process, but this learning process is limited to an "oral" dialogue between students under the role of teachers' learning profession.

The rationalist philosophical basis of the collective individual learning model is that people acquire knowledge by thinking, reasoning and using logic and that people acquire knowledge by practicing their brains. The collective individual learning model organizes information in the brain in the collective. The collective individual learning model lacks the philosophical standpoint of empiricism. In the "nine one" classroom culture, it is difficult for students to have the knowledge that is revealed by empiricism equal to experience. The collective individual learning model lacks the philosophical basis of empiricism. The collective individual learning model has the characteristics of formal collectivity and substantial individualism. It is not only the general learning mode of Chinese school classrooms but also the Western individualistic cooperative learning mode which is fundamentally different from the Western learning theory. This paper puts forward the concept of the collective individual learning model and tries to get rid of the Western educational experience to understand the learning model. It is unfair to regard the historical experience of Western education in Europe and North America as the universal experience.

Therefore, collective individual learning mode also has profound historical roots, which comes from the traditional Chinese sutra learning mode and private school learning mode. In the collective individual learning model, teachers and students establish an interactive relationship mainly through language and thinking. Language is almost the only tool in the collective individual learning model. In the collective individual learning model, the construction of the learning relationship between teachers and students through the medium of language reflects that learning is a kind of three basic relationships of exploratory activities. The relationship between students and teachers, and between students and students is reflected in the interaction between students, teachers, and students. The relationship between students and society is manifested in the relationship and contradiction between students' individual needs and social needs. If the above three kinds of relations are established only through the medium of language, then the thought connection between students and teachers is extremely important. What we are going to talk about is, is there a way of learning through the relationship between students and things? In fact, the earliest human learning is to learn to use "natural tools" and then learn to make tools, which reflects the relationship between people and things. With the development of human experience, thinking, and language, mutual communication becomes possible, and learning in interpersonal communication becomes the main way. There needs to be pointed out that under the "nine" the classroom culture characteristics of collective personal learning has obvious Oriental social learning common characteristics, under this kind of characteristic, the proposed learning community can be understood, because it is trying to want to break through the collective personal learning mode, and true to the learning mode of community. He tried to build a learning community model to change the collective individual learning model, in essence forming a process of the community learning model. He tried to change the collective individual learning in the east. In his opinion, collective individual learning has uniformity, passivity, and individualism, but should change to the autonomy, initiative, and cooperation of learning.[6]

Variations of the collective individual learning model. We can understand collective individual learning as individual collective learning. If we understand collective and individual learning independently, we can construct two concepts of individual learning and collective learning. This means that there are four types in the logic of the relationship between collective and individual, namely collective individual, individual collective learning, collective learning, and individual learning. This means that collective learning carries out collective learning, individual collective learning carries out collective learning, and individual learning carries out individual learning. In collective individual learning mode, we can also be understood as a collective individual language learning of individual and collective of mathematics learning, collective scientific learning, collective, individual's moral learning the art of individual and collective learning, collective, individual sports learning, collective, individual learning to read and write the values of individual and collective learning. The "nine-one-centered" collective individual learning model is mainly the learning of complex psychological processes, which is mainly the learning of problem-solving or concept formation, and of course, there is also the learning of speech, namely reading or spelling, and there is little learning of perceptual-motor skills.

We can also distinguish the three types of collective individual learning according to the three aspects of knowledge, technology, and mind: collective individual spiritual learning, collective individual technical learning, and collective individual knowledge learning, spiritual learning, technical learning, and knowledge learning and their three kinds of mixed learning. Collective individual learning is usually produced in mind without an utilitarian purpose of the listener, in the church, Buddhist temple, ancestral hall, hall, and other public places, collective sermons, pennant. Xuan Daohe said that, the ideological and moral education in Chinese education system doesn't focus on examining the learning tools and measurement approaches. There are two kinds of logic in collective individual technology learning. One logic is technology as a learning tool to promote learners' knowledge learning, and the other logic is technology as learning content to promote learners' ability to use technology. While the collective individual technical learning of the latter logic is carried out in specialized classrooms through "technical" courses, the collective individual technical learning of the latter logic is not reflected in classroom classrooms. As a result, we will create a new kind of classroom culture, classroom culture beyond

---

[6]Yu Wensen. Ten lectures on effective teaching [M]. Shanghai: East China Normal University Press, 2009:187–201.

information technology hegemony, information technology and equipment of the classroom culture becomes the mainstream trend of the development today, but for not students section of the students, we need to create a technology based on human civilization provided by the different technologies of classroom culture, rather than a single information technology classroom culture. To change the "nine one" classroom culture, to create a variety of types of classroom culture. Collective individual knowledge learning generally exists in the "nine one" characteristic classroom culture. It is a unique human learning paradigm to explore knowledge and truth. It is a learning paradigm to promote learners' cognitive development with textbooks as knowledge carriers, a pen and an exercise book or exercise book as personal learning tools.

The social development value of collective individual learning

No matter what kind of learning pattern should achieve the ultimate goal to promote the development of students, obviously collective personal learning for students development should create value, and students' development is various, such as brain development, physiological and physical development, cognitive and emotional development, moral and civil development, personality and social development, health and safety development, and the development of art and aesthetic, collective personal learning will affect many student developments, and play a role. Here we focus on the value of collective body learning for students' social development. Collective individual learning is the main means to promote students' social self, social development, and individual development. The question is, how does it promote the social development of students? In form, students' development is based on self-growth and individual, but social learning is not enough for social cognitive ability, social–emotional skills, social development, moral development, and civic development. Therefore, collective individual learning needs a collective division of labor, reflecting collective cooperation of learning and collective responsibility of learning. Collective individual learning needs to form a real collective, because only the real collective spirit to support the learning of the students, to make the collective trust, only in the study of collective trust among middle school students can get a happy learning experience, can realize the student individual in collective implementation ego, which can give out consciously altruistic behavior, rather than competitive exclusive learning behavior. Collective individual learning also reflects the relationship of "free association of human beings". "individuals are free in their association and through this association... The free development of each is the condition of the free development of all." That is, the "union of free men" of learning, which also confirms the view that "we can only exercise our freedom in cooperation with others, which is only an appreciation."

How does collective learning give way to individual learning in collective individual learning? If collective individual learning wants to play the role of collective learning, it needs to learn division of labor, because only in collective behavior can there be the division of labor, and cooperative learning must be realized by a clear division of labor. Collective individual learning is the learning of students' division of labor and cooperation. For students, the division of labor is equivalent to the division of labor, so it reflects the characteristics of sharing. Collective individual learning without the division of labor cannot achieve the goal of collective learning. "Sharing is the spiritual communication and material redistribution of the members of the collective, showing the mature collective of" organic unity." The sharing of collective individual learning should be based on spiritual and material communication, while the existing "nine one" classroom culture cannot provide this foundation. In collective individual learning, the spontaneity or guidance of the division of labor depends on the teacher's learning design in class. The spontaneous division of labor will enable students to realize the true meaning of the division of labor. Students will volunteer to do things and learn and experience happiness and happiness in the process of doing things. In the collective division of labor in learning, students can cause positive changes in cognition and emotion by doing things, so as to promote sharing and communication resonance with peers and realize the conscious altruistic behavior of learning trust and learning.

Collective individual learning should unify the process of collective learning with the result of collective learning or combine the process of collective learning with the result of collective learning (learning evaluation). The collective learning process alone cannot promote the social development of students. As mentioned in article, professor advocates that "learning community" is mainly in the Eastern countries education is characterized by "nine" classroom culture, it is keen to see the eastern classroom culture to promote students' development and the limitation of the study, because students in "nine" as the characteristics of classroom culture cannot be used to promote the development of students' social environment. There is no question of students' individual learning, because the final academic achievements are based on "personal" for statistics, any kind of test, in the end, is done in the name of "personal", so the individual learning is usually the sign of god's truth, but the problem is that in our classroom, most of the study is based on "collective individual learning performance, its effect on students' academic achievement how much? This is an unsolved mystery."Collective education" and "education in the collective" are two different concepts, the former is to cultivate students' collective consciousness through collective education, the latter is to educate in the collective education, this kind of education can be any content of education, "collective individual learning" is the performance of "education in the collective". The traditional school education "could be divided into dozens of people a group of students, more than a dozen people, 'into' size of space of the classroom, by a teacher in charge management, in order to form a brain in the fastest time, moving in tandem, ideological unity of the collective cohesion" understanding does not conform to, because in collective individual learning mode, the students are learning in a collective way, although each student is "unaware" of the individual existence, but the personal characteristics of classroom culture show students' personal learning.

2.5 The Conclusion

This chapter uses the concept of "collective individual learning mode" instead of "collective individualistic learning mode" concept, also it doesn't use the "mass personal learning model", the reason is that using the "collective individual learning mode" is a kind of research found that is not a claim that more than one argues that because there is no teacher or the principal claims to be in the classroom teaching is a kind of collective personal learning mode. The Chinese classroom learning models always follow Western learning theories. Sato has been trying to create a community learning theory different from the west, but without talking about individualism or opposing individualism. I think there should be a learning theory based on the objective facts in China. It is psychological, historical, ethical, political, cultural, and aesthetic. It should be realistic. It should reveal the difference between the classroom culture and Western culture in China, in our opinion, this is to understand the performance of the most significant difference between Chinese and Western school education content, but with the deepening of the understanding of the problem, the paper raised the mode of collective personal learning concept, the demand of its theoretical construction is put forward, and theory can explain the phenomenon, and for education, it is the biggest bottleneck problem for solving China's education today, namely to cultivate innovative talents and their correlation. Based on the understanding of the above two aspects, our question is whether the collective individual learning model proposed in this paper can reveal the uniqueness of Chinese education in the micro field. The question is how to cultivate innovative talents under the collective individual learning model? Collective individual learning mode is mainly expressed in the "nine one" classroom culture. To what extent can this classroom culture cultivate innovative talents?

This study strives to pursue a goal of creating a theory, usually, "scientific theory has two important aspects, (1) the form of the theory, including the theory contains words and symbols; (2) the empirical aspect of theory, including the physical events that theory seeks to explain." In terms of form, the collective individual learning theory includes the discourse of collectivism, individualism, learning, etc. In terms of experience, it includes collective individual learning to explain the physical events of students, teachers, curriculum, and teaching as well as the environment contained in Chinese classroom space education. In addition, the new curriculum reform has been discussing classroom reform, learning style reform, and other issues related to student learning. In the discussion, some scholars have proposed the basic characteristics of the new curriculum learning style, including initiative, independence, uniqueness, significance, communication, experience, question, and innovation. The question is what kind of classroom culture are these basic features of learning? The further question is, to what extent do these basic features manifest themselves? Some scholars have proposed various types of learning, such as knowledge learning, operational learning, communication learning, reflective learning, observation learning, practical learning, etc. The question is how these learning types are realized in the classroom culture characterized by "nine ones". Can they be embodied in collective individual learning? To what extent can the science of learning be applied to collective individual learning? More specifically, how can learning science be used in the "nine one" classroom culture? How can learning core concepts or keywords in science, such as design research, learning communities, constructivist learning environments, cognitive apprenticeships, conceptual transformations, case-based reasoning, model-based reasoning, and computer-supported collaborative learning, be applied to collective individual learning models? "Nine one" classroom culture has many limitations for promoting student development, so it is necessary to open up student learning spaces in addition to "nine one" classrooms, such as natural space, laboratory and experience space, including woodworking room, metalworking room, sewing room, and so on.

Even in the "nine one" classroom, the culture should go beyond the current space focusing on the cultivation of cognitive ability, and develop the culture of students' self-care ability, such as cleaning, cooking, garbage sorting, lunch giving, etc. Traditional culture education is not only about reading classics, but also experiential education, such as story course, stage play, flower ceremony, tea ceremony, martial art, calligraphy, painting, etc. All these traditional culture education needs to go beyond the "nine one" classroom culture. The collective individual learning model is far enough to only learn in the classroom environment, it needs to be educated in nature, that is, to implement collective individual learning model in nature, so that students get imagination, curiosity, and other creativity necessary for training. In my opinion, the sources of creativity are mainly nature, history, and intuition, which are partly based on nature and history. The influence of the classroom cultural environment is on the children's brain development. What is the relationship between brain neuron development and classroom cultural environment? What is China's distinctive education? What does it do to children's brain development? China's collective individual classroom culture emphasizes discipline, leading children to "mature" prematurely, showing early self-control and obedience. Based education reform at present, introduced the concept of "shifts", in fact, teachers and students in class and class from the perspective both exist at the same time.

Tthe current class system refers to the teacher's room, students walk shifts, and students in the room, traditionally teachers go shifts, because in the past, do not walk in chamber is made of the teachers and students class system, but because of either in class or leave class, eventually make teachers and students of the relationship between teaching and learning, go shifts while embodies the stratification of students and learning content, but not fundamentally change the collective personal learning mode.

Chapter 3
Analyzing "Collective Individualism Learning": Implications and Values

This chapter puts forward the urgency and the necessity of construction of classroom culture, classroom culture problems leading to education reform cannot succeed, by only transforming the classroom culture we can get rid of the plight of the education reform, classroom culture is the student studies the guaranteed rights culture, classroom culture is the most basic condition of students to learn effectively carried out; Second from students' physiological and physical development, cognitive and emotional development, moral and civic development, personality and sociality development, health and safety, the point of view of the needs of the development of art and aesthetic connotation of classroom culture building, and then discusses the promoting teachers' professional consciousness change and the transformation of the students to learn the value of classroom culture, finally proposed based on school culture, teachers' self-knowledge, discipline, and study period, such as information technology classroom culture builds the path.

3.1 Introduction

Whenever I am in the classroom of Chinese schools, I always think of a problem: we have studied almost every aspect of education that can change, from the curriculum to the core qualities of students, and then the classroom where students study every day is surprisingly quiet in research and policy. We need to think carefully: what is the relationship between the classroom and the problems encountered in the development of education in China today? No students, no teachers, just a desk, a chair, a blackboard, a projector, and a computer. How do students in classrooms with only one textbook, one exercise book, and one pen experience learning difficulties? Or is there no relationship between students' learning difficulties and the classroom? At a time when the point of blame is all exam-oriented education, whether it is the heavy burden of students (heavy homework burden, only the exercise book burden), or lack of creativity cultivation, does it have nothing to do with the classroom? How is the relationship between teachers and students established in a classroom that is almost

© Springer Nature Singapore Pte Ltd. 2020   29
X. Zhu and J. Li, *Classroom Culture in China*, Perspectives on Rethinking
and Reforming Education, https://doi.org/10.1007/978-981-15-1827-0_3

empty except for the cold physical space? Is the only teacher–student relationship with the help of textbooks, notebooks and exercise books? Do students only listen, speak, and do exercises in the classroom? Can't they play and work? Can't students work with material materials? Do all the desks and chairs in the classroom have to be the same? Can't there be a bigger round table for a few students to sit around and discuss? The questions are endless, but they force us to identify "classrooms" as research objects.

In the past decade, the kindergarten, primary schools, and secondary schools paid much attention to building playgrounds, libraries and dining halls with less focusing on creating classroom and campus culture at different contextual background. Set at the same time, in the past few years I gave myself a task, it is has the opportunity to access to foreign universities and I must visit the school of the basic education, from kindergarten to high school, and in the visit an assignment, is to observe the different school classroom, therefore also gave himself a "classroom culture" view, obviously intent on, use this concept to observe the classroom, my colleagues and I also wrote an article. I visited the United States, Britain, Japan, Singapore, and other countries of the classroom after school, and found that the classroom culture of the same and difference exists obviously, first not to discuss the obvious difference in different countries education classroom culture is how it affects students' learning and development, just exist in a static classroom culture to analyze the relationship between students' learning and development is also an very interesting issue.

The differences between Chinese and foreign cultures obtained from the observation of school and classroom culture forced me to think about many questions. If so, what causes the differences between Chinese and foreign cultures in school culture and classroom culture? So the question that we're going to ask further is, what kind of classroom culture do we need to build? Why build classroom culture? How to construct a classroom culture? This paper mainly discusses the classroom culture of elementary education, especially compulsory education and high school education.

3.2 The Urgency and Necessity of Constructing Classroom Culture

Today's basic education reform in China is no more urgent and necessary than the construction of classroom culture because the problems of classroom culture have led to the failure of education reform. Classroom culture is the culture that guarantees students' right to learn. Classroom culture is the most basic condition for students to study effectively.

The problems of classroom culture lead to the failure of educational reform
The government is the top-level designer and promoter of education reform. Therefore, it is impossible to attribute the failure of education reform to the government. Schools are the implementers of education reform, and they are also carried out according to the roadmap designed and guided by the government. Therefore, schools

cannot be blamed for the failure of education reform. Society and family are only auxiliary forces for education reform, but they are not the leading forces for the failure of education reform. Objectively speaking, the failure of educational reform is not a lack of ideas. The ideas and theories of educational reform proposed in each period are also scientific, but why can't they always be effectively applied in practice? In this way, almost all factors affecting the failure of education reform are excluded. The question is what factors lead to the failure of education reform? Here we propose that the failure of educational reform can be attributed, at least in part, to the problems of classroom culture.

From what we have observed about the classroom culture of Chinese schools, the contents of decorative school culture, posted school culture, slogan school culture, and plaque school culture are generally displayed. These school culture has obviously impact on producing innovative learning ideas and communicative skills for students on campus. The issues we found today are that school education can be explained by the problems existing in the classroom culture and quality education to carry out effectively in class is not significantly important reason is that the classroom culture of "poor", the basic education curriculum reform implementation is not ideal in class object is the cause of classroom culture of "desolation", students' development of core accomplishment if unable to promote the root cause is possible in class classroom culture of "poor", on the other hand, if you want to make Chinese education out of today encountered many difficulties need to China's "cultural revolution" in the classroom, the school made the classroom culture "abundance", "wealthy", and "rich".

Only by reforming classroom culture can we get rid of the dilemma of educational reform

The most fundamental task of education reform should be to transform culture. In school education reform, the closest culture to teachers is classroom culture. If classroom culture is not reformed, it is almost impossible to reform education. Although great achievements have been made in curriculum reform after several generations of efforts, some old problems have not been solved and new problems keep emerging. Usually people are not successful due to the education reform "exam-oriented education", this is a misunderstanding on and because of the exam system is the prevalence of a system, no matter which country, through the test to measure students' academic performance, and ultimately choose talent is by far the most basic system arrangement of human, human beings cannot cancel the test for the success of education reform, we are always on the examination system and the reform could not change the education, and only by transforming culture can we truly achieve the road of education reform. But the cultural transformation should start from the reform of school culture, and the school culture transformation should start from the classroom culture transformation. Only after the school reform can the education reform be successful, and the school reform should be based on the school culture reform, further speaking, only the school classroom culture reform can the education reform be truly successful. The reason is very simple, true to successful education reform is the power of the teacher, the teacher in education reform has become a real power but a copy of teaching materials and teaching reference is impossible to play, only in the classroom rich culture can make teachers change their professional consciousness, the classroom culture and teacher's professional consciousness constitute a dialectical relationship.

Classroom culture is the culture of students' right to study guaranteed.

We should endow the classroom culture with the proper status and change from the traditional concept of "school equipment" to "classroom culture", so that the classroom culture has the cultural characteristics of students' right to learn. We believe that the classroom culture is the right of students learning, the richness of classroom culture is the basis of students' right to availability, classroom culture is a rich learning resource for students of a state, this state directly determines the rights of students to learn more or less, the classroom culture is part of the students to create the culture, is the student creative performance. Building classroom culture should not only play a role in educating students but also provide students with the right to learn. It is hard to imagine how a "sterile" classroom culture with only one textbook, one notebook, and one pen can guarantee students' full right to learn. For example, what we can't stand is that only one instrument gives all students the right to learn music. Why Chinese students study so hard? Because the classroom culture in Chinese schools is so barren. In the absence of a rich classroom culture, it is impossible to guarantee students' personalized learning in the classroom. Without a rich classroom culture, it is impossible to carry out situational learning, which is emphasized by learning science. Without rich classroom culture, students cannot carry out project learning, inquiry learning, and cooperative learning, let alone cultivate students' cognitive ability of problem-solving.

Classroom culture is the most basic condition for the effective development of students' learning

How does learning happen in the classroom? What activities do students learn in the classroom? What conditions do students need for learning and activities to take place in the classroom? Only to accept learning methods and activities, then simply take the book or teaching classroom culture is enough, the problem is that students learn to operate, observational learning, reflective learning, practice learning, inquiry learning, and cooperative learning different ways of learning activities and then only in textbooks, textbooks, and exercise books, notebook as the main material culture of classroom culture is able to meet? We rarely discuss the students' choice of operational learning, inquiry learning, cooperative learning, and other learning activities or ways, what kind of classroom culture should be provided for students? If this problem is not solved, how can students learn to change? How to solve the problems existing in basic education? Why are teaching aids rampant? The reason is that students have no other conditions for learning in class except teaching materials and auxiliary materials. Some experts strongly call for the cancelation of the publication of teaching materials. The question is what will students learn after the cancelation? If there is no rich classroom culture, how to let students have the conditions to learn. Poor classroom culture results in unhealthy students. Poor health outcomes, such as poor vision and obesity, are closely related to poor classroom culture. We need to encourage students to actively communicate with different peers to enrich their insights and enhance their cooperative learning skills through participating campus activities. The concept of classroom culture reminds us to "pay attention to their lives, needs and desires in the present", and we can no longer regard "children's life status, needs and desires as a warning of adult life, as a threatening social problem to be solved". What are their immediate lives, needs, and desires at school? It is safe to say that when they are in the classroom at school, their life is not just a textbook sitting on the desk and chair life, their needs are not just listening to the teacher, their desire is not in front of parents and teachers to test a high score record, the question is what is the current life, needs, and desires of children?

3.3   The Connotation of Classroom Culture

Changing classrooms are nothing new to schools today. The room is described in some media revolution: "the classroom is not a consisting of tables and chairs and a blackboard material space, more should be full of diverse physical space, warm living space, full of fusion information space and more force of social space, can the ecological culture of space, and to change the classroom space let this multivariate the realization of the spatial ability." The problem is that if the classroom space of diversity, warmth, integration, multi-strength, and multi-capability is not a cultural classroom, then it is no more than a physical space without educational significance. It seems that it is very necessary for us to construct the connotation of classroom culture.

   First of all, classroom culture must be the material, spiritual, institutional, and behavioral culture to meet the needs of students' development, and the culture to meet the needs of students' physical and physical development, cognitive and emotional development, moral and civic development, personality and social development, health and safety development, art and aesthetic development. Therefore, classroom culture should be a culture that aims to construct students' development goals. Classroom culture refers to the culture of students' physiological and physical development. Classroom culture should not only follow the rules of students' physiological development but also meet the needs of students' physiological development. For example, the material culture of the classroom should design diverse desks and chairs according to the different physiological development needs of students' bodies, which should reflect the characteristics of different demographies. Classroom culture must be directed to students' cognitive and emotional development. Classroom culture should reflect the needs of students' cognitive development, should reflect the characteristics of the thinking process, and should be a rich material environment in line with children's cognitive rules. Classroom culture should also reflect students' emotional development and be conducive to students' emotional expression. Classroom culture must be directed to the development of students' morality and citizenship. Empty classrooms fail to cultivate students' moral character and civic responsibilities, obligations, and rights. How can you train a moral and responsible citizen in a classroom with only one textbook and only one teacher to tell you? The concepts in textbooks can enhance students' moral and civic cognition, but cannot form students' moral feelings, will, and behavior. It fails to cultivate the civic quality of students' rights, responsibilities, and obligations. Classroom culture should provide institutional culture and material culture for the development of students' morality and citizenship. For example, there should be national flags erected, hung, and displayed in the classroom, rather than only pasted with national flags. Classroom culture must be directed to students' personality and social development. But at the same time, the social development of students can be guaranteed in the system culture of the classroom. "To socialize means to learn how to be human, first by mastering social norms and making them self-conscious, and second by learning how to properly handle and adjust interpersonal relationships and integrate individuals into society". The classroom is the culture for students to learn to be a good person. Classroom culture should be the action system of teachers and students, which can provide a normative culture for students' development. Classroom culture must point to the healthy and safe development of students. The formation of school health characteristics and the provision of safe classrooms all point to the healthy and safe development of students. Classroom culture must be directed to the development of students' art and aesthetics. Classroom culture should provide a rich material culture for students' artistic and aesthetic development. Chinese schools usually have "special classrooms" or "professional classrooms", such as a computer room, dance room, music classroom, art classroom, etc. On the one hand to provide students with rich art and aesthetic material culture, on the other hand, to show students' art and aesthetic development of creative culture.

Classroom culture should be the spirit, material, system and behavior culture of students' learning, and classroom culture should be the culture created by students' learning environment. Students learning performance for resources logic of knowledge learning, learning, communication operation, observation, and reflection, is characterized by way of logic learning, autonomous learning, cooperative learning, inquiry learning, experience learning, digital learning, such as, in addition to the book learning, acceptance learning, all types of learning activities and learning needs on the basis of the culture of the classroom. How can we operate, communicate, observe and learn without a classroom? How can we operate, cooperate, explore, experience, and learn independently?

We put forward that learning science should be taken as the basis for the establishment of classroom culture. How can project learning, inquiry learning, cooperative learning and situational learning around learning science be carried out in the classroom? If there is no classroom culture, how to develop students' problem-solving skills? Provide students with an alternative learning environment for personalized learning, and design a classroom system culture for students' cooperative learning. The prerequisite of students' personality development is personalized learning, which needs corresponding personalized learning conditions. Classroom culture should provide abundant material resources for students' personality learning.

The classroom is the learning space for students and the space for teachers to teach students to learn. The classroom culture is the space culture or cultural space for students to learn. This space should not be blocked by doors and walls. Then, classroom culture is the spirit, material, system, and behavior culture created by teachers and students together. Classroom culture is the value system of a concept level, in accordance with the relevant cultural value system of thought, the classroom culture should be a concept of value and standard value and the practical value of the unified value system, induced by the teachers and students behavior motivation, guidance and restriction of action between teachers and students, so that the behavior of teachers and students from the individual level of the free will based on conflict of disordered, shift to the orderly and harmonious collective level, to keep the classroom in the "order" state. Classroom culture is a kind of classroom "order", it is the meaningful behavior of the action of teachers and students, is the direction of the action of teachers and students, and has the function of unifying the action of teachers and students to make it become the order of teaching and learning. Action is due to people's inner beliefs, ideals, norms, and other 'meaningful' ideas—values—acting on people, thus making people's autonomous behavior on the basis of perception, cognition, namely thinking and judgment, and thus forming the subjective order. The classroom culture should be a continuous spiritual, institutional, material, and behavioral culture of family culture suitable for children's growth. Classroom culture should be children growing life culture, it is an extension of family culture, children in the rich classroom culture "eat, drink, and be merry", hungry can eat food, thirsty can drink water on time, can lay on the ground reading a book, can provide the stage for children's improvisational performance, can also have a television, can even go to a toilet at any time, and need not rush to the class if it is crowded in the toilet. Classroom culture is "education is life" culture. In short, the classroom culture construction should be the premise of students' development and learning, and in the education field of vision, student development refers to the students in the process of accepting education for physical, cognitive, and emotional, moral and civil, personality and sociality, health and safety, artistic and aesthetic aspects of the quality and quantity of positive changes a process and state. Classroom culture should be a culture that promotes student development and learning. The classroom has the interactive meaning of time and space only when students, teachers, and culture coexist. Classroom culture is a culture that provides students and teachers with learning and teaching, a culture where students can actively, independently, and subjectively construct the learning process, and a culture where teachers can realize the whole professional attribute.

3.4   The Value of Constructing Classroom Culture

Classroom culture promotes the change in teachers' professional consciousness
There is a basic assumption that is true, that is, the success of education reform

depends on whether teachers' professional consciousness changes in the classroom. Only when the teachers' professional consciousness changes, can the educational reform take place, and the educational reform can be successful. What are the factors that lead to the change in teachers' professional consciousness? Our point of view is the construction of classroom culture. The classroom culture exists in the form of materialization. Both the classroom spiritual culture and the classroom system culture show the materialization form. This is also consistent with the basic principles of Marxism. Matter determines consciousness as the basic principle of Marxist history and dialectical materialism. In fact, the diversity of classroom culture can be understood by cultural materialism, because classroom culture ultimately reflects the cultural substance in the physical space of the classroom. Cultural substance refers to the materialized form of human culture, including the material actions of human beings and their achievements. We use the concept of "professional cultural material" to refer to the concept of the professional field. It refers to the materialized form of human professional culture, including the material actions of professionals and their achievements, which are perceived professional cultural things with material entities. Obviously, teachers' professional cultural substance refers to the materialized form of teaching professional culture that teachers may use in the professional field of the classroom. It is teachers' material action and results, and it is a tangible thing with the professional culture of education and teaching. From this, we can establish a new relationship, that is, the relationship between teachers' professional material and professional consciousness. The question is what is teacher professional awareness? According to the author's understanding of the professional connotation of teachers, the professional consciousness of teachers refers to the reflection on the professional connotation of teaching students to learn, educate, and serve. Specific refers to the consciousness of teachers' reflections on their professional practice, mainly including teachers to own existence significance, and how his reflection of the basic problems such as, including teacher's discipline knowledge construction consciousness, the knowledge construction of development of the students and the consciousness of learning, professor of consciousness, education environment consciousness, and the consciousness of their own development and so on. Classroom culture is the first in a culture material, with the teacher's professional consciousness exists between closely linked, when we put the classroom culture as a cultural material existence, it needs to discuss this kind of cultural existence and the relationship between the teacher's professional consciousness, can inference is that the classroom culture material existence determines the teacher's professional consciousness, on the other hand, teacher's professional consciousness affects the classroom culture, which is the basic theory of Marxist material determines consciousness substances exist in the classroom culture and the relationship of teacher's professional consciousness the application of the building. What we need to discuss further is that classroom culture should promote the change in teachers' professional consciousness. Therefore, it is necessary to reconstruct the classroom culture to promote the reform of teachers' professional consciousness.

Constructing classroom culture to promote the reform of students' learning
The ultimate touchstone of the success of educational reform must be whether students' learning changes? Therefore, the construction of classroom culture should promote the reform of students' learning. How do students learn? How does learning happen in the classroom? How do students learn deeply in the classroom? Student learning cannot happen without classroom culture, let alone deep learning in the classroom. In the in-depth study, for example, that only active and meaningful learning is deep learning, reflective and critical thinking ability training as the goal, to cultivate students' innovative ability in the process of problem-solving, such deep learning objective need to deep learning process to ensure that, so the diagnosis "with autonomous learning achievement attracting students, with rich experience of cooperative learning to attract students, to explore the mystery of learning to students, the emotional communication with learning draws students", the problem is how to develop students autonomous learning, cooperative learning, inquiry learning, emotional communication? There will be empty talk without classroom culture. There is no shortage of ideas, but classroom culture, because without classroom culture, teachers, and students cannot achieve deep learning. Promoting students' learning reform must depend on students' perception of classroom culture, subject culture perception, system culture perception, material culture perception, and spiritual culture perception. When culture and cognition are connected, we can better understand that students can have better cognitive development when they study in the classroom culture. When students are learning based on cultural perception, what should teachers do? Only when teachers have the knowledge of cultural perception and design the learning environment for students can it be effective. This puts forward two propositions of classroom culture, one is students' learning based on cultural perception, and the other is teachers' professional awareness based on students' cultural perception. Only in the classroom cultural perception can students cultivate their creative ability, in other words, if we want to improve our creative ability, we need to transform our classroom culture. Classroom culture must be conducive to the cultivation of students' innovative ability. It is required to build classroom culture according to the requirements of "cultivating creative attitude, enhancing understanding of creative process and creative characters, training creative behavior and creative thinking, and teaching specific creative skills."

An important symbol of promoting the students' learning reform is the students' personalized learning. The question is how does the classroom culture create the conditions of personalized learning for students? Obviously, classroom culture should be a spatial environment suitable for students' personalized learning. In the classroom students try to carry out personalized learning needs the corresponding conditions; this condition is the classroom culture. Personalized learning is not only the individual learning of each student with a textbook and a book but also based on the diversity and the culture that is conducive to students' personalized learning. One of our basic judgments is that no matter how teachers construct students' learning content, they cannot only learn in the "nine one" classroom culture. On the contrary, because classroom culture is "nine one" culture, teachers' professional consciousness can only be played in the "nine one" professional cultural material conditions.

The question is, can students learn any content only in the "nine one" classroom culture? It can be concluded that different learning contents should be conditioned by different classroom culture.

3.5 The Construction Classroom Culture Pathway

The construction path of classroom culture based on school culture

From the perspective of relations, classroom culture is constructed on the basis of school culture, and it is directly restricted by the reasonable relationship between "goals and means" in the process of school culture construction. We can pursue diversity. The question is what is the consensus goal?, of course, is to promote students' development, the school culture should take the student development and learning as the logical starting point, if the student development as the logical starting point to understand the school culture, so the composition of the school culture must first have basic knowledge of student development, this awareness should become an indispensable part of school culture, and even can think so, no student in the development of school culture does not exist, so schools should be for students to have a basic understanding, to describe the connotation of the development of students. Classroom culture should be built on the cognitive framework of school culture for students' development and learning.

Classroom culture is constructed through the public foundation of school culture. It is not only the cell of school culture but also the reflection of school cultural diversity. The publicity of school culture is reflected in the public area of the school, while the diversity of school culture is reflected in the classroom culture. As mentioned above, classroom culture is also an integral part of school culture, which is mainly reflected in the multi-level classroom culture. It should not only reflect the publicity of school culture, but also reflect the administrative hierarchy of school culture, but also reflect the individuality of classroom culture. Classroom culture is created by teachers and students. Classroom culture is the extending and deepening of school culture, it is not decorative culture and school culture, but created by students and teachers, it is advantageous to the student to study, and reflect the students' learning, is to see, should be a reflection of the students' learning outcomes, the students learning results were eventually reflected in school culture and classroom culture. The classroom culture is constructed by the physical culture of the classroom. Through the classroom the physical space of the construction of material culture, make children learning based on color, can touch, size, length, height, hard, and soft attributes of the object, this is the source of physical knowledge says Piaget, it is the source of empiricist claims that experience knowledge acquisition, secure, by the characteristics of consciousness through see, touch, play with children gain knowledge of these properties. "The object itself and the physical action of the child towards it are the sources of physical knowledge."

Classroom culture construction path based on teachers' self-knowledge formation

As indicated above, classroom culture is created by teachers and students, and the construction of classroom culture cannot be separated from the role of teachers. The construction of spiritual culture, institutional culture, and behavioral culture in classroom culture should be realized by the class teacher and the science teacher. And the role of teacher is reflected through the formation of teachers' self-knowledge, thus to build the path of classroom culture is the formation of teachers' self-knowledge to form the core part of the teacher is the teacher's students to develop self-knowledge, the classroom culture obviously depends on the formation of teacher's students to develop self-knowledge. We can even think that the core of the creation of classroom culture lies in teachers' self-construction of students' development knowledge. The question is how teachers form the core of classroom culture through the self-construction of students' development knowledge.

Classroom culture is built by the teacher–student community. For students, classroom culture is the reflection of their academic achievements in the learning process and learning results, as well as the agreements or class rules and systems negotiated by students and teachers. However, for teachers, classroom culture is a part of their self-knowledge construction. Teachers are the most important constructors of classroom culture. Such as positive emotional culture construction: call students name, say please and thank you, smile, and love. The key is that teachers must understand the components of students' positive emotions. In fact, we find a serious problem in our communication with teachers, that is, teachers have the only experience in the cognition of emotions, not understanding, let alone how to construct students' emotional elements in the classroom culture. Similarly, to promote students' cognitive development, moral development, civic development, social development, and safety development through classroom culture, teachers must first construct their own knowledge of cognitive development.

The construction path of classroom culture based on discipline and learning segment

Classroom culture has strong discipline and learning characteristics, academic features of classroom culture is mainly manifested in the different classroom culture construction of different disciplines, it is obvious, such as classroom culture should be based on the arts to meet each student's art learning for the purpose, so you need to provide every student of art appreciation, experience the creation of the art equipment, it is not simple and equipment for the tool, is a kind of material culture, and be in harmony of the classroom. Other disciplines also reflect the characteristics of students' learning classroom culture, as long as the classroom culture created for students' learning, no matter which kind of classroom culture is valuable. Classroom culture is also reflected in the learning of students' learning characteristics, such as the kindergarten classroom culture branded with the imprinting of early childhood education experts thought, compulsory education phase of the primary school for kindergarten classroom culture also create the characteristics of the primary school classroom culture, discipline characteristic is apparent, and the high school classroom culture more reflects the academic culture, discipline culture become a concept, is to build in the field of academic culture, such as the humanities, social sciences, natural sciences, art, language, etc. Our country in this respect shows less obvious differentiation, from high school is based on a specific subject to build the school culture, which directly determines the cultural differences in the classroom, we basically couldn't reflect the academic culture, even if there is the culture of academic discipline is relatively fragmented, we can see that the geography classroom, history classroom, physics laboratory, artificially separated in the field of comprehensive academic disciplines. What needs to be put forward here is that our schools, especially middle schools, have formed two kinds of institutional arrangements, namely, the student class system and the class system, which directly raises the question of how to construct the classroom culture.

The construction path of classroom culture based on technology
Technology should not only refer to information technology but also include agricultural technology and industrial technology. Therefore, the path of classroom culture construction based on technology mainly includes the path of classroom culture construction based on information technology, industrial technology, and agricultural technology

1. Construction path of classroom culture based on information technology. With the application of the Internet and other information technologies in traditional classrooms, classroom culture has also changed. Therefore, we put forward the path of constructing classroom culture based on information technology. The construction of classroom culture based on information technology first faces how to provide students with an environment where real learning resources and virtual learning resources coexist? iPad and other technologies provide classroom cultural opportunities for classroom digital technology culture or information technology culture, increasing students' learning resources from the past unitary real learning resources to the dual coexistence of virtual learning resources and real learning resources. However, our classroom is in a state of relative poverty, poverty, and poverty of real learning resources. Therefore, it is under double pressure to build the classroom culture of real learning resources and virtual learning resources. However, we need to point out that no matter how we construct classroom culture based on information technology, students' learning and development benefits should not be harmed. The so-called "flipped classroom" objectively extends students' learning pressure to their families and must be carefully used. We can see the future is that the construction of classroom culture must be the blended with culture of network culture and classroom culture.

Construction path of classroom culture based on industrial technology
Classroom culture construction of industrial technology means that industrial technology accumulated by human civilization becomes an important part of classroom material culture through material objects, specimens, micromodels, etc. It is not only the classroom culture for students to learn technology, but also the means and tools for students to learn knowledge and subject knowledge. China's bridge technology, water conservancy technology, transportation technology, construction technology, and other technologies have reached the world level, and these technologies can be used as tools for students to learn by means of miniaturization model or "parts", and can also become means for students to understand the subject knowledge and explore the truth.

The construction path of classroom culture based on agricultural technology
When information technology enters the classroom and becomes part of the culture, we really need to discuss, for students, is information technology an end or a means, and if it is both an end and a means, what is the end? What are the means? Compared with farming techniques and industrial techniques, what are the similarities and differences between them in promoting students' learning and development? It also reminds me of the role of farming skills in growing up as a child. I live in a mountain village. I have never been out of the mountains before I went to high school. As far as I can remember, my work included cooking on a stove, herding cattle, cutting grass, planting rice, mowing the field, digging grass, pulling weeds, cutting rice, planting vegetables (wheat, potatoes, corn…), and climb trees, cut wood, and even carry a load, especially carry firewood, the stream, the water pool to swim, catch fish in the river, ditch dug, eel, loach can do more than 20 with adults in the home all the year round and some snacks, and acquaintances society, relationships between people in the village, the traditional game between friends, or even in the dark of the night go to the mountain, at that time, all these farming skills are for the benefit of the home, let the family can eat rice, household, or even pay for tuition, this is the purpose, but became the means of growth and the growing process is full of and nature and harmony, such as earth. Farming skills are no less valuable to human growth than industrial and information skills.

3.6 The Conclusion

Today we discuss the classroom culture, as education researchers we feel ashamed really, the reason is that more than 100 years ago, in the school and society, Dewey keenly observed, "organization for the knowledge of physical teaching, no matter how many can never replace about farm and pastoral direct knowledge about plants and animals, this knowledge is directly on the intimacy and plants and animals and care for them in the process. The discipline of sensory training in schools for the purpose of training can never compare with the sensuality and richness of life expressed in a familiar career". Dewey was not satisfied with the physical teaching of classroom learning in the school reform brought by the Industrial Revolution. He also noticed that schools carried out sensory training, but he was not satisfied. The question was how to build classrooms into places where students could really learn without abolishing classroom learning in schools. Dewey said, "schools have the opportunity to connect themselves to life as a home for children; Here, children learn by living directly." "The typical homework activity adopted in schools is free of any financial pressure and is not aimed at the economic value of the product, but at developing children's social skills and insights". Apparently, Dewey hoped that the classroom of the school should be the place for students to live. Instead of taking notes and doing homework with exercise books and workbooks, students would learn to do homework with raw materials. Isn't that the classroom culture we are talking about today? As I mentioned in the article introduction, we are in a school for the United States after a classroom observation of written by the American classroom culture is originally is a reflection of Dewey's thoughts, and we also studied the Dewey, about 100 years, but not reflected in our classroom, don't the Chinese traditional culture to Dewey thought in classroom culture reflect the soil? We only know class teaching system of the Industrial Revolution, but I don't know class classroom culture of the Industrial Revolution change, need to have a rich culture to support the Industrial Revolution brings to the requirement of talent cultivation, namely Marx about the all-round development of people should have a "comprehensive" quality. Today, the industrial society and the information society coexist in the post-industrial society, and we still have Dewey's words in the state of "if we imagine the common classroom, there are rows of ugly desks arranged in geometric order, all of which are piled together, and the space for activities is extremely narrow; A desk of nearly the same size, barely big enough for books and pencils, with a lectern, a few chairs, and perhaps pictures on the bare walls, allows us to recreate the only educational activity that took place in the place. It is all about being able to 'listen'—because simply learning the lesson in the book is just another kind of listening, which creates the dependence of one mind on another. A listening attitude, by contrast, implies negativity and absorption". From the "nine ones" classroom culture, we pointed out above, don't you think it still stays in the era of the classroom culture described by Dewey 100 years ago? We advocate the concept of classroom culture. On the contrary, we should abandon such concepts as "teaching aids", "equipment", "teaching resources" and "learning aids". We also advocate that the concept of classroom culture should gradually integrate "special classrooms" or "professional classrooms" with ordinary classrooms, instead of setting up special classrooms.

Chapter 4
Reviewing Classroom Culture: Perspectives from Chinese Scholars

This chapter focuses on offering a review of classroom culture from the studies on the Chinese context. It mainly involves the definitions of class culture, Chinese current studies on classroom culture, the construction of classroom culture, and the Chinese development stage of classroom culture research. All these sections contribute to analyzing the review of classroom culture from the studies of the Chinese context.

4.1 The Definitions of Classroom Culture

"Class" is the basic organization for students to receive education at school, and is the main carrier for students to self-educate, manage and serve. The basic unit of the school is the class, and the class is also an important group for students to learn in the school and an important place for life. The class is the first important group organization that students come into contact with except the family.[1] Class culture is an important component of campus culture, and also a source of vitality for the campus culture.[2]

Class is an educational organization. The class of modern school is related to the establishment of class teaching system. The class of modern school is related to the establishment of class teaching system. In the seventeenth century, the Czech educator Comenius not only summed up the practical experience of class education at that time but also theoretically clarified the school education organization system. In the "Large Teaching Theory", he puts forward : "all children in Mandarin schools

---

[1]Da Jianlong. High school class culture Practice Strategy of Construction [A]. Compilation of Scientific Research Achievements of Research on Teacher Education Capacity Building (Volume IX) [C]: Institute of Educational Science, Chinese Academy of Management Sciences, 2018:4.

[2]Wu Honghua. Exploring the relevant construction strategies of class culture [J]. Guangdong Sericulture, 2018, 52 (9):110–111.

© Springer Nature Singapore Pte Ltd. 2020   43
X. Zhu and J. Li, *Classroom Culture in China*, Perspectives on Rethinking and Reforming Education, https://doi.org/10.1007/978-981-15-1827-0_4

are required to spend six years in school and should be divided into six classes, one classroom per class, if possible, so as not to interfere with other classes." He said each class is a grade, "class" and "grade" are closely linked.[3] From individual teaching to class teaching, it is not a simple collection of many individuals, but a qualitative change in school educational activities. According to modern sociological theory, social groups become social organizations once they have clear organizational goals, clear organizational goals, strict organizational structures, and strict organizational norms. As a formal group, classes usually have their specific members, specific goals, specific cultures, specific interpersonal relationships, and their specific functions. Therefore, the class is a school education organization composed of a group of students of a certain age stage and the level of development, and the school takes the class as the basic unit to carry out a variety of educational activities.

The characteristics of classroom

As the grassroots organization of school education and different from other social organizations, the class has the following characteristics[4]:

Classes aim to promote the overall development of students

Any social organization has its own goals. The goal of class organization is to promote the overall development of students. The students in the class play the role of "learners". whose basic task is to learn. There are not only explicit courses designed in advance, such as teaching subjects, but also recessive courses in various aspects of class organization, such as norms, roles, interpersonal relationships, and so on. It is the class organization that provides an environment of collective life for young students, which plays an important role in promoting the socialization and individuation development of students and highlights the educational nature of the class to its members.

Class composition has a number of stipulations

As far as the class organization is concerned, in terms of personnel traits, the members who constitute a particular class are limited in age and culture, that is, the level of physical and psychological development is roughly similar, and the level of knowledge is roughly the same; in terms of size and number of people. The number of students in each class is generally fixed. That is, in the process of accepting a certain type of education (except for special reasons), the number of students in a class is relatively stable; in terms of standardization and order, the class has strict rules and regulations. And the various norms and orders are basically stable; in the time limit, the class composition time is more than a specified period of time, usually from the beginning to the completion of a certain stage of educational tasks.

---

[3] Wang (2013, pp. 1–4).
[4] See footnote 3.

The direct and multifaceted communication between teachers and students in a class

A direct face-to-face interaction between teachers and students in class organization. From the perspective of teachers, teachers must exert a targeted influence on students after they understand the characteristics of students, the current state of mind, and the level of understanding of the content of teaching. The cognitive strategies that teachers take on students will have an impact on the activities of students in the class, especially the interpersonal relationship between teachers and students, which is extremely important in class management and student knowledge. The interaction between teachers and students in the class organization also has many sides. In the actual class activities, the interaction between the class teacher and the teacher and the students, and between the students and the students are often multifaceted, with knowledge transfer and acceptance, as well as emotional communication and sharing. In implementing these functions of the class, there are both the relationship between the teacher and the student, the formal role between the student and the student, and the various informal relationships between them. Therefore, the class teacher and the teacher should pay attention to the extensive interaction with the students through various channels, and promote the in-depth interaction between the students, so as to achieve the goals and functions of the class organization in the process of meeting the needs of the class subjects.

The immaturity of class members

Students who are members of the class are in the process of physical and mental development. Although their level of development varies greatly depending on the age of the students, the students are immature among the members of the society as a whole. Therefore, the class must rely on the strength of the teacher to a certain extent, and it is impossible to implement complete student self-management. On the one hand, students have a certain degree of dependence on teachers or class teachers in schools, especially when they are frustrated by their own strengths. It does not disappear completely, but the degree of dependence varies with age; on the other hand, although the student is not an adult, his sense of autonomy is a near-natural social requirement, and as he grows older, the sense of autonomy will gradually increase. Many studies have shown that even the first graders of primary school have begun to seek independence in school life since the day of enrollment.

Emotion is the bond of the class

Emotion is an experience that reflects the relationship between the subject and the object. The healthy development of the class organization depends to a large extent on the emotional state of the class teacher and the teacher, and the degree of cognition and understanding of the class members based on this. The art of education for class teachers and teachers is to make the class organization have a great attraction to students, so that students have a sense of yearning, honor, and friendship for the class so that the students' good performance can be cultivated in the class organization. Class teachers and teachers should handle the relationship between non-mandatory means such as rules and regulations, discipline, and other non-mandatory influences such as professional rights and personality demonstrations, and firmly grasp the emotional ties between class members and establish interactive and mutual trust with students. Harmonious interpersonal relationships improve the efficiency of class activities and promote the achievement of class goals.

Culture

"Culture" is an objective existence that has a subtle influence on individuals and groups. Under the influence of different cultures, people will form different life attitudes, values, and different behaviors.[5] British anthropology, cultural scientist Taylor defines culture in his masterpiece "Original Culture" as a complex whole, including knowledge, beliefs, art, law, morality, customs, and the talents that humans acquire. China defines the term "culture" as the combination of "text" and "enlightenment". Such as Han Liu Xiang, "Say the Court, refers to the Wu": "If a wise person manages the world, he will first use the morality to educate the world and then use force to conquer the world. But if you use force to conquer the world, the nationals will not be convinced with you. If you use the morality to govern but you can't change it, you can punish him." The virtues and cultivation, therefore the definition of "culture" is more inclined to the human aspect. In modern research, Chinese scholar Zhang Dainian gave a more accurate description of culture in the book "Chinese Culture and Culture", that is, "culture can be seen as a process in which people interact with their surroundings." The way of communication and the overall results created in the communication; "Ci Hai" defines culture as: in a narrow sense, it refers to the ideology of society and the institutions and organizations that are compatible with it. The more widely recognized in China is the definition of culture in "Ci Hai".[6]

Class culture

"Class culture" has been one of the key research subjects in the field of sociology research in the Hengwei class in the 1920s and 1930s, which has aroused the widespread concern of Western education scholars. Chinese educational researchers have different views on the study of class culture. Wu Honghua thinks that class culture is influenced by different social culture, campus culture, family culture, and the ideal belief, values, outlook on life, attitude to life, mode of thinking, etc., which are formed in the process of learning and communicating with class members under the influence of class culture.[7] Da Jianlong summed up the class culture as: Class

---

[5]Wu Honghua. Research on the related construction strategies of class culture [J]. Guangdong Sericulture, 2018, 52 (9):110–111.

[6]Da Jianlong. Practice strategy of high school class culture construction [A]. "Research on Teacher Education Capacity Building" (Compilation of Scientific Research Achievements (Volume IX) [C]: Institute of Educational Science, Chinese Academy of Management Sciences, 2018:4.

[7]Wu Honghua. Classes Research on the related construction strategies of culture [J]. Guangdong Sericulture, 2018, 52 (9):110–111.

culture can be considered as an important branch of social culture. Class culture is an important part of campus culture. Class culture should be led by class teachers, and all members of the class should participate in it. [8] Zhang Mingmin and Zhang Xiaohua.[9] The class culture is influenced by social culture and campus culture. Teachers and children have a purposeful and systematic creation of material culture and spiritual culture that meets the requirements of social development and their own development needs. Li Zhendong believes that class culture refers to the spiritual wealth and culture created and formed by class teachers and students through education, teaching, and management activities under the guidance of the class teacher. Enclosure and the form of activities and material forms that carry these spiritual wealth and cultural atmosphere.[10] It is defined as: Class culture is a broadly influential activity for teachers to shape students' character through the creation of class mental goals, class systems, class environment, class activities, etc. But this overview highlights the status of the teacher and neglects the student's main role[11]: Institute of Educational Science, Chinese Academy of Management Sciences, 2018:4. Different scholars understand the class culture from different perspectives. In this study, the definition of class culture is followed by the Dictionary of Education. That is to say, class culture can be referred to as group culture, and class culture should be the common belief, common value orientation, and common attitude of the class group.

Classes are the main place for students to acquire knowledge. Classes are the places where students learn the most during their study life. Students in the school will develop a certain world outlook, outlook on life and values, which will have an important impact on students entering the society in the future. Good class culture helps students to learn and grow. Good class culture plays a prominent role in promoting students' coordinated development and adapting to social development: excellent class culture can enhance students' ability to adapt to society and strengthen students' inner morality. Feelings can help to regulate behaviors and conduct behaviors.[12] Healthy class culture construction can not only effectively mobilize students' interest in learning and practice, but also enable students to form good moral character, shape a positive class spirit, infect students with a good cultural atmosphere, and promote students' healthy growth. Once the class culture is created and formed, it in turn condenses, stimulates, guides, and controls the students' behaviors, which make the students' thinking, study, and life change greatly.[13] As the saying goes: "One who stays near vermilion gets stained red, and one who stays near ink gets stained black."

---

[8] See footnote 6.

[9] Zhang Mingmin, Zhang Xiaohua. Reflections on the Construction of Junior Middle School Class Culture—Taking Qushui County Middle School as an Example [J]. Tibet Education, 2018 (10):61–63.

[10] Li Zhendong. Problems and countermeasures in the construction of class culture [J]. Gansu Education, 2018 (21):42.

[11] Da Jianlong. Practice strategy for high school class culture construction [A]. "Research on Teacher Education Capacity Building" compilation of scientific research results (Volume IX) [C].

[12] Jiang Meiying. Class culture construction model and innovation research [J]. Journal of Jiamusi Vocational College, 2018 (4):304.

[13] See footnote 10.

It can be seen that the impact of different environments on the development of people, the impact of different environments on human development is different, the impact of this results are also different. For students, a school is a place where students study and live for a long time. The difference in the school environment plays an important role in the growth and development of students. Different environments will have different developmental effects on students. Therefore, creating a good campus environment and class environment is crucial to the development of students.[14]

Students usually study and live on campus as a class. Create a good educational environment for students, so that students can truly feel that this is a happy place to learn and live. The cultural construction of the class is not only the construction of a cultural atmosphere but also a process of shaping the physical and mental development of students. Class environment construction cannot directly look at a form, not only to fulfill the school's class management requirements, it must be correct, feasible, and motivated. The difference in the cultural environment of a class has a significant impact on the future development of a student. The content and form of the educational curriculum are diverse. Among them, class culture education is a special method of education, and it also plays a particularly important role and effect.[15]

4.2   Chinese Current Studies on Classroom Culture

4.2.1   Characteristics of Classroom Culture

At present, the research on the cultural characteristics of the class is more convergent to the study of its function. The two have a close relationship, which is mainly reflected in the following aspects:

Collective
The class name is based on the "collective". This requires the starting point of all members' actions to create a colorful class culture under the collective interests and perspectives. At the same time, the class as a group, the construction of its culture is not completed by the class teacher alone, it needs to give fully attention to the group internal students, substitute teachers and other groups to cooperate and build. In "A study on the Construction of Class Culture based on the characteristics of Primary Schools", Dai Lei said: "Class culture is the wealth created jointly by all the teachers and students in the class, the crystallization of the common work of all teachers and students, and the teacher in charge of the class together with all the students." The

---

[14] Kang Kai. On the importance of class culture construction [J]. Tianjin Vocational College Joint Journal, 2017, 19 (3):115–118.

[15] See footnote 14.

Educational practice of promoting the growth of students through the Construction of Class Life.[16]

Social

On the basis of Dewey's conclusion that "education is society", some scholars put forward that we should pay attention to "The nature of society" in the construction of class culture, and its core idea is "to make schools a microcosm of society and to form a close connection with society." "To enable students to realize the needs and values of society in school, and to acquire knowledge and life skills from mutual experience with society".[17]

Normative

Some researchers believe that: "The normative class culture represents the collective thoughts, wishes and interests of all members of the class, and has a normative function for the whole class of teachers and students." The individual's thoughts, psychology, and behavior should at least be the collective ideal of the class. The thinking, psychology, and behavioral methods of aspirations and interests should be consistent with the goals, concepts, thoughts, psychology, and behaviors of the class—to be consistent with the class culture.[18] Some scholars also pointed out: "After the formation of class culture, it has a clear directivity, standardizing the behavior and concept of each class member".[19]

In addition to the above three characteristics, some scholars have proposed that the class culture has the following characteristics: "subjectivity, uniqueness, positiveness, dynamics, etc." Li Wenping pointed out the class culture in the article "The Content and Characteristics of Class Culture Construction". "Direction, education, innovation, etc."[20] Liu Hongyun in "Class Culture Construction". A brief discussion on the class culture has "penetration". In the "Class Culture Construction Research", Lu Yuyu pointed out that class culture has the coexistence of dependence and independence, the coexistence of passive and active coexistence, the coexistence of explicit and implicit coexistence, the plasticity and the difficulty of coexistence.[21] Another scholar believes that class culture is characterized by the combination of science and ideology, the combination of pluralism and unity, the combination of stability and plasticity, and the combination of independence and openness.[22] In

---

[16]Dai Lei. Research on class culture construction based on the characteristics of primary school sections [D]. Suzhou University, 2011.

[17]Original Qinglin. Dewey and Ikeda's "school function" view and its enlightenment [J]. Journal of Zhaoqing University, 2009, 30 (4):57–60.

[18]Wang Qian. Junior high school class culture under the new curriculum concept Construction practice and research [D]. Yanbian University, 2010.

[19]Ye Weifang. Class culture construction Practice and Reflection [J]. Ideological and Theoretical Education, 2012 (8):6–60.

[20]Li (2004, pp. 23–24).

[21]Lu Yuyu. Research on class culture construction [D]. Guangxi Normal University, 2005.

[22]Pei Chunyan, Liu Dongfeng. On the culture of class Significance, Characteristics and Construction [J]. Journal of Taiyuan Institute of Education, 2004 (S1):232–233.

addition, regarding the characteristics of class culture, some researchers believe that it is mainly reflected in the following aspects[23]: First of all, class culture is an open and inclusive culture. In the student's learning career, many activities are basically completed in the class. The class members participate in the whole class during the whole school, whether they are studying or participating in any activity. Over time, the various ideas, hobbies, and interests of class members may be assimilated by members of the same class, so the class culture is a relatively open and inclusive culture. Members can embrace each other and integrate with each other. Second, class culture is an equal culture. Every class member is equal, so the class culture should also be equal. In this cultural circle, members come from different places, different families, and environments, but it does not affect the equal integration of members into the cultural circle of this class. Everyone has the same right, which means that they have to bear the same Obligation. Finally, class culture is a culture of change. People themselves are social bodies, people will change, and people's thoughts and thinking will change. Therefore, the class culture will also change accordingly, so we must learn to face different cultural atmospheres and strengthen our ideological and moral construction.

4.2.2 Classroom Culture Functions

The class culture is a spiritual culture expressed in the style of class, study style, values, interpersonal relationships and public opinion, and the corresponding material culture. It affects every child subtly. Class culture plays an important role in the development of the class and the growth of students.[24] The function of class culture was carried out. Summary mainly includes the following points:

Condensation and infection function
The class belongs to an organizational form, which has a certain cohesive force. The main performance of the class culture maintaining the class cohesion includes that the class members can work together in learning, and can be related to each other in life, help each other, and coordinate in action. The specific class culture will inevitably have the effect of cohesion and infection. It can integrate and integrate the diverse cultures of different social culture, family culture, and campus culture brought by the class members, thus forming the overall class style of the class characteristic. The cohesive and infectious function of class culture can maintain and strengthen the cohesiveness of the class, which can help the establishment of the class team and help the team spirit of the class.[25] The class culture closely links the growth of

---

[23] See footnote 12.

[24] Zhang Mingmin, Zhang Xiaohua. Some thoughts on the construction of junior high school class culture—Taking Qushui County Middle School as an example [J]. Tibet Education, 2018 (10):61–63.

[25] See footnote 2.

individuals and the development of classes to form a "community of destiny". Class culture is a collective culture created by all members, bearing their common ideals and pursuits, embodying their common psychological awareness and values; this will motivate their recognition of class goals, norms, and pride as class members. Feeling, sense of belonging, and then form a strong centripetal force, cohesiveness and class collective consciousness.[26]

Education and guidance functions

As an invisible educational force, class culture deeply influences every member of the class. Class culture, such as the quiet spring rain, nourishes the children's hearts, embodies the children's sentiments, and shapes the children's souls. The education and guiding function of class culture is mainly manifested in the ability to cultivate people's comprehensive qualities and abilities. First of all, to enhance the realm of people. Because class members accept different cultures such as campus culture, family culture, and social culture during their growth, their principles of action and thinking in the initial class interpersonal interactions are different. These differences will lead to class members experiencing embarrassment, conflicts, collisions, contradictions, and then subtle influences, and eventually begin to follow the common class interpersonal rules. The process of this change is the process of the class culture, and it is the process of class members thinking about major issues in the class culture. Second, purify the soul. The society is full of all kinds of temptations, and guiding students to consciously resist bad temptations and keep the purity of the soul is the most important issue for educators. Class culture has a non-utilitarian value orientation, which is guided by spiritualism, highly praises and carries forward value rationality, and purifies the human mind. Third, train people's thinking ability. The common method of constructing class culture is to carry out thematic educational activities, which can train the thinking ability of class members. In addition, the empowerment of people. Class culture construction process will carry out a variety of activities, these activities can provide a stage for students to show talent, so that students can develop talent, optimize students' comprehensive quality. Finally, class culture can also cultivate sentiment and shape people's character. In the class culture, class members will not only be influenced by the humanistic spirit, but also by the material environment and ideas. These factors will enable students to receive spiritual and spiritual comfort and encourage students to develop a positive and enterprising spirit.

Specification and constraint functions

Class culture is a normative system that restricts the words and deeds of every member. Everyone's words and deeds need to be consistent with the mainstream culture of the class, and then accepted by the class. The healthy and civilized class culture is inseparable from the normative constraints of organizational discipline, and the class system culture is an important component of class culture. The class system culture

---

[26]Zhang Mingmin, Zhang Xiaohua. Some Thoughts on the Construction of Junior Middle School Class Culture—Taking Qushui County Middle School as an Example [J]. Tibet Education, 2018 (10):61–63.

is mainly divided into tangible rules and regulations and intangible institutional culture. Although the latter is not written, it shows the traditional habits of the class. The norms and unwritten rules contained in the class culture "flexibly" manage each student, so that they can voluntarily practice the rules and ethics of the class, and thus form a psychologically compatible, harmonious, and orderly class atmosphere. Class members not only need to abide by written and tangible rules and regulations, but also follow the class traditions and habits that the class members have agreed upon and form together. In the class system culture, students need to make constant choices between active compliance, passive observance, self-discipline, and other laws, and gradually form good morality that obeys the rules and regulations and is strict with self-discipline.

Harmony function
Class culture is a bridge between class members and a link between their hearts. It is helpful to have good communication, friendly cooperation, and harmonious function among class members. Class culture can promote class members to achieve ideological, behavioral harmony, but also help class members to build learning, life harmony.

Incentive function
The affiliation and recognition of each member to the class encourages them to actively contribute their own "positive energy" to the class's honor and to the development of the class. In this process, they further enhanced their sense of pride and identity toward the class, and then continued to motivate them to contribute to the class and contribute their own talents.

4.3   The Construction of Classroom Culture

4.3.1   Theoretical Basis of Class Culture Construction

Da Jianlong proposed the theoretical basis of class culture construction mainly on the following aspects.[27]

Multiple intelligence theory
The famous psychologist Gardner believes that human beings have at least eight kinds of intelligence, namely: language intelligence, mathematical logic intelligence, spatial perception intelligence, physical exercise intelligence, musical intelligence, interpersonal intelligence, self-recognition intelligence, and natural observer intelligence. And each person's different potentials correspond to these eight kinds of intelligence. The core of the theory of multiple intelligences is to promote students

---

[27] See footnote 6.

to learn through inquiry and cooperation, and to make each student's wisdom shine in common inquiry activities.

Self-organization theory
Self-organization theory is a new theory in the field of education management that has just emerged in recent years. A reasonable and orderly structure will be created to adapt to the external environment and even to the external environment. The great significance of self-organization theory research is that it can solve the problem without the external force, and the problem can be solved reasonably through the cooperation of related functions within the system itself, so that the various resources of the system can be optimally utilized. The theory of self-organization is based on the respect of human emotion to meet the basic needs of human beings and constructs the structure of the organization in order to maximize the utilization of organizational resources. Under the guidance of self-organization theory, the class teacher should give full play to the main function of the students in the construction of class culture. Through the self-management of the students and the timely guidance of the head teacher, the class should develop toward a positive and healthy direction.

Dual-subject cooperation theory
In the field of educational theory, the important characteristic of the definition of subject education is that teachers play an important guiding role in the process of education and teaching. However, teachers should respect the existence of students and play the role of students in education and teaching activities in the process of driving education. The role of the main body is the premise, aiming at perfecting and developing the subjective personality of the students, cultivating the subjective ability of the students, and promoting the overall healthy development of the students' personal qualities. Subject education is the practice of quality education, which reflects the connotation and basic ideas of quality education. Teacher Zhan Wansheng put forward the concept of "dual-subject cooperation theory". He believes that the status of teachers and students is equal. Both are the main subjects of educational activities. Students should not be in a passive subordinate position. Teachers should give students more participation in education. Opportunities for activities can use appropriate methods to stimulate the development of students' main functions in educational activities. Under the guidance of the dual-subject theory, the development of class culture should adhere to the active guidance of teachers and the active participation of students to effectively promote the smooth implementation of class culture.

Forms of class culture construction

The expressions of class culture include class material culture, class behavior culture, class system culture, and class spirit culture. From the morphological point of view, the class culture consists of the concept layer, the system layer, and the visual layer. Among them, the concept layer exists objectively, and the core content of the class culture concept is the class style. The institutional level can be directly felt by people and is the foundation of class culture. The main content is the class system culture. The class concept has an important influence on the construction of class culture, and it is also the basis of the class system and image. The class concept determines the content of the class system and class image.[28]

Material culture

The visual embodiment of the material living environment of the class is the hygiene of the class, and the good sanitary environment is the foundation of the construction of the good material living environment of the class. Therefore, when constructing class material culture, strict health system should be formulated to cultivate good hygiene habits of class members.

Behavioral culture

No activity, no class. In all kinds of activities, the understanding between members is deepened, and the cooperation with each other is more familiar and tacit. In the process of working together to achieve common goals, the children's sense of belonging and honor to the class has gradually increased, and the cohesiveness of the class has gradually improved. During the activity, the class teacher seized the opportunity to educate the children in time, strengthen the children's awareness of the rules, collective consciousness, and give the children the attitude of success or failure and learn to adapt to the new adjustments. In the activities of the times, the children's consciousness of "rise or fall together" is continuously strengthened, and gradually consciously conscious of the honor of the class and consciously abide by the rules and regulations of the class, making the class better and better.[29]

Institutional culture

Class system culture is the foundation of building a class style, and a good institutional culture is a prerequisite for the formation of a good class style. To this end, building a class system culture is of great significance to the construction of class culture. The institutional culture of the class should be fully considered to ensure the effectiveness of the class system and to fully demonstrate the class characteristics. After the class system is established, it should be implemented and implemented for a long time.

---

[28] Wu Honghua. Research on the related construction strategy of class culture [J]. Guangdong Sericulture, 2018, 52 (09):110–111.

[29] See footnote 26.

Spiritual culture
The definition of class spirit is the belief, thought, and code of conduct that are commonly recognized in the class formed by the class during the development of the school. The construction of class spirit culture is the focus and difficulty of class culture construction. Class spirit is the soul of class culture and has a guiding role in class system culture and material culture construction. Class activities are a common method of building class spirit.

Principles of class culture construction
From different perspectives of scholars, they offer various kinds of guidelines as follows[30]:

Advance with the times, highlighting school characteristics
The construction of class culture is carried out under the influence of social culture and campus culture. On the one hand, the construction of class culture needs to keep pace with the times and conform to the mainstream culture of social development. On the other hand, it needs to match the development orientation and characteristics of the school itself.

In line with the student's cognitive level and knowledge structure
The construction of class culture should conform to the age of students and the accumulation of existing knowledge.

Highlight the excellent culture of the nation and respect the national customs and habits
In the class culture, it is necessary to integrate the excellent traditional culture of the Chinese nation, so that children can witness the excellent culture of the nation in their study life, improve their aesthetic ability, and strengthen their perception and identity of outstanding national culture.

Full participation, brainstorming, and focusing on the role of cadres
Class culture construction is a systematic project. It needs to integrate the wisdom and talents of each member. It requires everyone to actively participate in it, and can gradually improve and gradually mature. Therefore, in the process of construction, teachers and children should give full play to their strengths, contribute to the construction of class culture, optimize and develop gradually; in this process, everyone participates and deepens the relationship between students and teachers. Understand and discover the advantages of each other and accelerate the integration of the class.

Influencing factors of class culture construction
Researcher Wu Honghua believes that the influencing factors of class Campus culture have a decisive influence on class culture. It is the development of class culture and the

---

[30]Zhang Mingmin, Zhang Xiaohua. Some thoughts on the construction of junior high school class culture—Taking Qushui County Middle School as an example [J]. Tibet Education, 2018 (10):61–63.

construction of the environment. It is also the source of class culture progress. Campus culture requires that the content of class culture can respond to it. The continuous promotion of campus culture will make the class culture change simultaneously. The construction of class culture is influenced by the law of education. The construction of class culture should adapt to the law of the physical and mental development of students. It is consistent with the training objectives of the class; although the construction of the class culture needs to follow the same general requirements, there are differences between the different classes, so the adjacent classes will affect each other.[31]

Problems in the construction of class culture

The construction of class culture refers to the process in which class members (including teachers and students) purposely and systematically create material wealth and spiritual wealth in accordance with social development requirements and their own development needs. Therefore, the construction of class culture should fully consider the integration of internal and external factors, but at this stage, despite the further deepening of the new curriculum reform, the attention to class culture construction has been continuously improved, a Campus culture has a decisive influence on class culture. It is the development of class culture and the construction of the environment. It is also the source of class culture progress, but for a variety of reasons, class culture construction has shown many problems to be solved in the development of the past decade.

The Unitality of the subject of Class Culture Construction

Some researchers believe that "class culture construction lacks democratic awareness, adopts paternalistic supervision, and neglects the cultivation of students' cooperative consciousness".[32] It is mainly reflected in the lack of students' subject rights in the class culture many cases, the class size and size affairs are decided by the head teacher alone, and the students are in a marginalized position in the construction of class culture because of the lack of acceptance of the students' opinions. In the current education, many class teachers usually use the traditional class management mode to carry out the class management work, standardize the students' behavior by the paternalistic way of education, and the teachers have not institutionalized the class management. There are few opportunities for students to participate in the democratic management of the class, the construction of the class culture is not deep enough, the influence and restraint of the construction of the class culture system are not brought into play, and the management mode of "Nanny type" ignores the subjectivity of the students, which is not conducive to the cultivation of the students' self-consciousness.[33] Similarly, under the current exam-oriented education model,

---

[31] Wu Honghua. The relevant construction strategy of class culture Exploration [J]. Guangdong Sericulture, 2018, 52 (09):110–111.

[32] Wang Qian. Practice and research of junior high school class culture construction under the new curriculum concept [D]. Yanbian University, 2010.

[33] Li Qing. Discussion on problems and countermeasures in class culture construction) [J]. Science and Technology Journal (mid-term publication, 2019 (2):173–174.

students are competing for their own development with fierce competition. Students have a small range of activities in schools, and the burden of schoolwork is heavy so that students are in a state of intense learning for a long time, and there is not enough time and the students cooperated and communicated. The teachers tend to pay attention to the students' academic achievements under the guidance of test-oriented education thoughts. They lack the awareness of the cooperation consciousness and the comprehensive quality training of the students. Cultivating students' sense of cooperation lacks comprehensive awareness, and the collective activities carried out by the organization are in the form, resulting in students not establishing a good sense of cooperation and lack of cooperation. In addition, some scholars believe that in the current educational environment, class teachers are accustomed to adopting the "class cadre appointment system" in class management, which makes most students unable to participate in the class culture construction. As a substitute teacher for other teaching subjects, it is in a state of "collective aphasia", which is expressed as the free state of "just take classes, regardless of other." Education is not an individual behavior. Similarly, the construction of class culture is not the sole responsibility of the class teacher. It requires the mutual cooperation and cooperation of the various subjects in a class environment.

Class culture construction is too formalized
From the horizontal perspective, the most common practice in the current class culture construction is to carry out a series of class activities, but the effectiveness of the activities is generally not high. On the other hand, most of the class activities are led by the head teacher, and the purpose of the activities is only to cope with the inspection of the units at the next level, which leads to the tendency of "not worthy of the name" in the development of the activities. On the other hand, due to the lack of understanding and understanding of the class culture construction, the class teacher cannot adapt to the students' needs. In most cases, it is in the form and fails to reflect its true connotation. In view of this, problems such as "shallow, random, hollow, and formalized" in the construction of class culture are inevitable.

The lack of systematic planning for class culture construction
From the perspective of the vertical dimension, some scholars believe that: "Class culture construction has a tendency of simplification, activity, fragmentation, and short-term. This tendency is mainly expressed as 'three weeks of heat'."[34] The class teacher is subject to certain influences to carry out class culture construction, but due to the lack of preparatory work in the early stage, it often makes the activities encounter obstacles, it is generally difficult to persevere. Pan Lishan believes: "At present, most of the cases about class culture construction are to organize materials horizontally according to class culture elements. Few organizations organize materials according to the vertical development of class culture from start to maturity."[35]

---

[34]Kim Lan. A study on the problems and Countermeasures in the Construction of Class Culture in Primary Schools [D]. Northeast Normal University, 2009.

[35]Pan Lishan. Research on problems and countermeasures in class culture construction [D]. Northeast Normal University, 2005.

Class material culture lags behind
Suhomlinski once said: "Whether it is planting flowers and trees, hanging picture slogans, or using wall posters, we will plan from the aesthetic level to explore its subtle educational functions and eventually even the school. The walls are also talking." Due to school funds, geographical conditions, etc., some students lack autonomy and persistence in their habits, and class environmental cleaning and environmental protection awareness are relatively poor [Li Zhendong. Problems and countermeasures in class culture construction [J]. Gansu Education, 2018 (21): 42].

The lack of creativity in class culture construction
As the main body of the class, students should be the direct participants in the construction of class culture. However, as far as the current literature is concerned, some scholars have pointed out that students are rarely seen in the construction of class culture, such as the most common board design and wallboard design and layout in the class. In most cases, the class teacher chooses some of them. Students with this specialty have to complete, and most of the remaining students have no chance to participate. Second, the design of these panels and wallboards is also based on some common templates. Few new designs emerged, lack of new ideas, and the indoor cultural layout of the class has often appeared in a uniform situation. For students who are growing up, thinking and creativity are greatly limited. In the long run, it is obviously not conducive to the development of students' creative thinking.

The lack of theoretical support for the construction of class culture
Wang Zhiyan and Kong Xiangyan pointed out in the question "The Problems and Countermeasures of Class Culture Construction": "Some class teachers often take action based on educational customs and personal experience when constructing class culture, but lack the consciousness to use relevant theories to guide their work." Zhou Yong pointed out: "The immaturity of the theoretical system is the root cause of the various kinds of 'virtual' behaviors in the class culture construction." It is true that China lacks education and training on teachers' class culture construction, which makes the teachers' theory lack. Starting from the teachers themselves, it is rare to involve reading some books on the construction of class culture, which makes the class culture construction in the actual situation greatly reduced in effect due to lack of theoretical support.

Pay insufficient attention to the consultation and counseling of student cases
On the basis of the above, Pan Lishan made a comprehensive and comprehensive description of the problems existing in the current class culture construction. She believes that in addition to the above-mentioned problems, the class culture construction lacks consultation and counseling for student cases. Each student is a unique living body. The problems encountered in the process of growing up are also different from person to person. The problems encountered by teachers in the process of building class culture are also different from person to person. Teachers are in

class. In the process of cultural construction, students' individual diversity should be fully considered. From the perspective of "all-people" or the educational concept of "life-raising", the class' own culture should be constructed to adapt the class culture atmosphere to the students' physical and mental development.

The lack of class culture personality
Education is aimed at the positive development of students' personality, but in the construction of class culture, many classes cannot find a "personality culture". In addition to the neglect of this work by the school, it is also due to the lack of initiative on the part of teachers. Lack of awareness of innovation and reform.[36]

In summary, the research on the problems existing in the construction of class culture, on the one hand, is reflected in the fact that teachers (class teachers) are separated from class development and student growth to engage in class culture construction, and to create a development vision of "air castle"; It is the students' mechanized absorption of various factors in the construction of class culture, and presents a class culture of "no soul". In view of this, only by taking into account all aspects of influencing factors, in order to make the various factors have a long-term coordinated development in the construction of class culture, at the same time, the class culture construction can truly serve the teaching.

Analysis of class culture construction strategy
In response to the problems existing in the current class culture construction, the researchers also put forward corresponding strategies. Li Qing believes that the construction of class spirit culture should be strengthened. The construction of class spirit culture is the core content of class culture and the concentrated reflection of the spirit of class personality. Establishing a good teacher–student relationship is conducive to promoting close communication and cooperation between students and teachers. Teachers should establish a correct concept of education, cultivate students' communication skills, establish an equal and friendly relationship with students, understand the needs of students, respect the personality of students, enter the inner world of students, establish a harmonious relationship between teachers and students, and promote to give full play to the overall effect of the class.[37] The school is currently the main front for cultivating and practicing the core values of socialism. Relying on the class culture as a carrier, it can effectively implement the value education into the daily teaching, effectively enhance the richness and profoundness of the teaching form, and enable students to internalize the concept of values into the heart and reflect it into daily performance, and then improve the effectiveness of education in the whole scope;[38] Li Zhendong believes that class culture can be promoted by creating a warm class material environment, building a democratic and open class system culture, carrying out meaningful class activities, improving student character, and encouraging

---

[36] See footnote 10.

[37] See footnote 33.

[38] Li Qing. Discussion on problems and countermeasures in class culture construction [J]. Science and Technology Journal (mid-season), 2019 (2):173–174.

self-development. Construction;[39] Lan Haiyan believes that the construction of class culture can be promoted by integrating traditional culture with class culture;[40] In the periodical and systematic engineering, the school as the main front of socialist core values education can combine the class culture construction with the socialist core values, relying on the class culture to better deepen the values education concept, thus enhancing the socialist core values. Influence.[41] Huang Huanqiang proposed that training a team of cadres who can do things, do things, and do good things is an important part of building a class team. However, the leadership and organizational skills of students are not born, but acquired by the day after tomorrow. Therefore, it is necessary to train the team of cadres. In particular, for the cadres of the cadres who are in the new post, the class teacher needs to have targeted individual open small stoves, and then send them to the horse to speed up their growth. After the cadres of the corps gradually become competent in the management role, the class teacher should be moderately invisible, build a platform for self-management of students, and gradually realize student autonomy.[42] Yang Wei believes that the essence of culture is "humanization" and "enlightenment". Humanization is the use of human standards and scales to change the natural behavioral process and its results, that is, to take care of people with all the practical experience and achievements of human transformation of nature. Cultivate people, upgrade people, and make people more "people." The class culture realizes "humanization" through various channels, and each member of the class is positively affected and grows and develops in the formed class culture, that is, realizes "enlightenment". To this end, class culture construction can be summarized as such a model: in the interaction with school culture, the class community has a long-term common run in the teacher–student interaction, life-long interaction, classroom teaching, theme activities, class life, and social practice. Adapt to each other and actively build, form unique class values, class conventions, ways of thinking, behaviors, and class environment to achieve "humanization." At the same time, each member of the class community is influenced by the culture of the class, promoted and changed ("cultural education"), and realized "humanization". Therefore, the construction process of class culture is a two-way interaction process of "humanization" to "enlightenment" and mutual correlation (Fig. 4.1).[43]

---

[39]See footnote 10.

[40]Lan Haiyan. Exploration on the Integration of Traditional Culture and Class Culture Construction [J].Primary School Teaching Reference, 2018 (33):85–86.

[41]Du Laiping. Class Culture and Socialist Core Values Education [J]. Literature Education, 2019 (2):177.

[42]Huang Huanqiang. Exploring the construction of high school class culture in the new era [J]. Huaxia Teacher, 2018 (33):87.

[43]Yang Wei. Model construction of class culture construction [J]. Education Vision, 2018 (19):4–7.

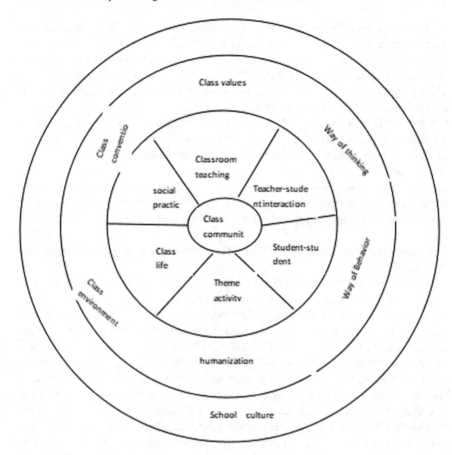

Fig. 4.1 Class culture construction model

4.4   Chinese Development Stage of Classroom Culture Research

China's research on class culture began in the 1990s, but it did not attract enough attention and attention from the academic community. Until the implementation of the new round of curriculum reform in 2001, the "class culture" gradually entered the field of researchers. Therefore, with the new curriculum reform in 2001 as a watershed, China's research on class culture is mainly divided into two stages:

From the 1990s to the beginning of the twenty-first century (2001 new curriculum reform)—the exploration stage of class culture research.
In the 1990s, class culture began to gradually separate from the field of campus culture research and received extensive attention from researchers, which led to the emergence of "class culture" research, on the basis of which many theoretical ideas and

works were derived. In the "Introduction to Class Society", Mr. Wu Lide conducted a theoretical exploration of the social culture model of the class from the perspective of educational sociology, and made a brief analysis of the elements and composition of the social culture model of the class;[44] Mr. Yu Guoliang pointed out in the "New Theory of School Culture" that in the process of building students' class culture, it is necessary to adhere to the combination of management and education, and to give full play to the important role of the class teacher;[45] Professor Li Xuenong, as a representative figure at this stage, systematically expounded the significance and nature of class culture research in "Secondary Class Culture Construction". It analyzes the composition of class culture and discusses the construction of class culture from the perspective of values, norms, and environment.[46] This stage is the exploration stage of the study of class culture in China, which lays a certain theoretical foundation for the study of post-class culture and plays a significant role in promoting it.

The new curriculum reform in 2001—the development stage of class culture research

Since the Ministry of Education promulgated the "Basic Education Curriculum Reform Program (Trial)" in 2001, there has been a new upsurge in class culture research in China. With the gradual advancement of the new curriculum reform across the country, it is imperative to establish curriculum standards and curriculum structures that are appropriate to the new curriculum system, and to adjust educational concepts and teaching methods. Therefore, the research on class culture has great innovations both in research content and in research mode. In the context of the new curriculum reform, class culture construction must show the characteristics of openness, democracy, interaction, and individuality. Wu Li focused on the relationship between new curriculum reform and class culture construction;[47] The components of the cultural environment were systematically analyzed.[48] In addition, many researchers have put forward many representative opinions on the class culture. The development of these theoretical researches and practical research provides guiding ideas for the construction of class culture in various colleges and universities in China after the new curriculum reform. It is suggested that the development of class culture research in China will be further promoted.

---

[44] Wu Lide. Introduction to Class Sociology [M]. Chengdu: Sichuan University Press, 1999:13.

[45] Guo Liang. New Theory of School Culture [M]. Hunan: Hunan Education Press, 1999:75.

[46] Li Xuenong. Middle School Class Culture Construction [M]. Nanjing: Nanjing Normal University Press, 1999.

[47] Wu Li. Research on class culture construction under the background of new curriculum reform [D]. Fujian: Fujian Normal University, 2007.

[48] Jiang Guangrong. Research on Class Social Ecology Environment [M]. Wuhan: Huazhong Normal University Press, 2002:8.

China's development characteristics of class culture research

Research attention continues to increase
In the past 10 years, the research on "class culture" has shown an increasing trend in terms of the number of documents, whether it is a master's thesis or a journal. It not only reflects the increasing attention of the academic circles in China to the study of class culture but also reflects the phased effects of the new curriculum reform in China. However, through statistical analysis of related literature, although the number of papers is increasing, the proportion of papers published in core journals is small, and the overall level of the papers needs to be improved.[49]

The scope of research objects continues to expand
The focus of previous research has mainly focused on the basic education stage (i.e., elementary school and junior high school, high school stage). After nearly 10 years of development, the class culture research on colleges and secondary vocational schools has also begun to flourish and become a research hotspot. The continuous expansion of the research object shows that the importance of the current class culture is continuously recognized, and it also lays a solid foundation for the study of class culture in the future.

The research field is gradually refined
At present, the study of class culture has gradually refined and formed an independent field. Scholars' understanding of the cultural connotation of the class is no longer limited to the framework of campus culture but is regarded as a special research category, and its functions and characteristics are gradually enriched.

Research model integration
Research on class culture has not only focused on the field of education, but also on various disciplines such as management and psychology. This research paradigm of multiculturalism not only injects fresh blood into the study of class culture but also expands the space of class culture construction, making the study of class culture a step further on the scientific road.

4.5 Research Methods are Relatively Simple

In the study of class culture, theoretical research and experience are mostly summarized, lacking in empirical and operability. Many scholars' research only stays at the processing stage of theory and data. There is less generative knowledge in the papers. Some scholars' researches involve certain case studies, but their records lack detailed and systematic. Therefore, in the future research on class culture, we should

---

[49]Feng Jiajia, Zhang Xiaowen. Retrospect and reflection: China class A review of cultural studies [J]. Modern Educational Science, 2017 (6):10–17.

pay attention to empirical research, and diversification of research methods is the correct development path of class culture research.

Therefore, although the research on class culture in China began in the 1990s, it began to attract attention with the implementation of the new round of curriculum reform. In the past 10 years or so, scholars have focused their research on the content, function, and characteristics of class culture, as well as the problems in class culture construction and related countermeasure research. Although some achievements have been made, the existing problems are still not tolerated. In the future research, we need to further deepen on the basis of reflection on the current research and strive to achieve multi-method, high quality, make the class culture construction return to life, and truly achieve student oriented.[50]

References

Li, W. (2004). The content and characteristics of class culture construction. *Teaching and Management*, (35), 23–24.
Wang, F., & Tang, H. (2013). *Construction and maintenance of excellent class collectives* (Vol. 1, p. 4). Wuhu: Anhui normal University Press.

---

[50]Feng Jiajia, Zhang Xiaowen. Retrospect and reflection: China A review of class culture research [J]. Modern Education Science, 2017 (6):10–17.

Chapter 5
Integrating Classroom Culture: Perspectives from Core Values of Chinese Socialism

This chapter involves integrating classroom culture from the perspectives of the core values of Chinese socialism. Specifically, the core value of socialism is an important part of socialism with Chinese characteristics in the new era. It is the dominant value or value system formed by the society under the socialist background. It is the core and foundation of the socialist value system. It concentrates on exploring the definition of China's socialist core values, development, and cultivation of socialist core values, and the connotation of socialist core values. The influence of socialist core values and its significance to the education and cultivation of Adolescent Values

5.1 The Definition of China's Socialist Core Values

The core value of socialism is an important part of socialism with Chinese characteristics in the new era. It is the dominant value or value system formed by the society under the socialist background. It is the core and foundation of the socialist value system. It is the basic value concept that our nation has followed for a long time to reflect the law and essence of socialist construction. It guides and supports our code of conduct and basic direction in the long-term practice of socialist modernization. Culture is the soul of socialist core values and the focus of socialist core values construction. What kind of culture will have what kind of values. General Secretary Xi Jinping once said that "core values are virtues in fact," and moral construction is the foundation of building a socialist core value system. Morality and culture are unified in the construction of the socialist core value system. They are the key to the construction of socialist core values and the soul and cornerstone of socialist core values. In the report of the 17th National Congress of the Communist Party of China (CPC), it was clearly stated that "we should integrate the socialist core value system into the whole process of national education and the construction of spiritual civilization, and transform it into the conscious pursuit of the people. We should actively explore effective ways to use the socialist core value system to lead the social ideological trend and take the initiative to do well in Ideological work, respecting

© Springer Nature Singapore Pte Ltd. 2020
X. Zhu and J. Li, *Classroom Culture in China*, Perspectives on Rethinking and Reforming Education, https://doi.org/10.1007/978-981-15-1827-0_5

differences, tolerating diversity, and resisting the influence of various errors and decadent ideas." This not only clarifies the educational function and function of the socialist core value system but also clarifies that it is an important task for the construction of socialist spiritual civilization to educate the people and cultivate correct values with the socialist core value system.

5.2   Development and Cultivation of Socialist Core Values

A society prevails in different mainstream values and cultures in different historical periods. On the one hand, this value culture inherits the culture and social accumulation of previous societies, on the other hand, it implies the new direction and needs of social development at that time. In the new historical period of contemporary China, our popular mainstream value culture is the core value culture of Chinese socialism. From the national, citizen and individual level, it puts forward the value development requirements for all walks of life, all levels, and all kinds of organizational units, from large to state machinery, enterprises, small to families and individuals. This value culture not only has guiding significance for the development of all aspects of the current Chinese society but also has historical adaptability and development prospects. The report of the Eighteenth National Congress of the CPC advocates prosperity, democracy, civilization and harmony, freedom, equality, justice and rule of law, patriotism, professionalism, honesty, and friendliness as the core value orientation of socialism. It is not only the inheritance of the past excellent ideas but also the summary of the great practice of socialism. It reflects the value pursuit of Marxism, but also the spirit of excellent national tradition. It also embodies the reference and tolerance of the value of modern civilization. The emergence of China's socialist core values has absorbed the ideas of the existing society, culture, and different historical periods, and has a profound historical origin. The ideological resources contained in the excellent Chinese traditional culture are: emphasizing self-improvement, harmony, patriotism, ethics, and peopleoriented. These thoughts are the deep source of the core values of socialism in contemporary China. The birth of Western utopian socialism also laid a part of the value foundation for the construction of the core values of Chinese socialism. Utopian socialists exposed and criticized the capitalist system, boldly predicted and demonstrated the basic principles of the future society, and put forward many progressive and guiding values of human history. Generally speaking, their beautiful vision and bold exploration of harmony, equality, democracy, labor, happiness, and all-round development of human beings constitute the main content of the core values of Utopian socialism. As one of the few existing socialist countries, China's social development and prosperity should embody the characteristics of socialism, while the previous scholars' statements on the values of the existence of utopian socialism naturally become part of the values pursued by China's social development.

The historical development of socialist core values has undergone a long process, which is mainly manifested in the transformation from fantasy to science, from theory to practice, from revolution to construction and reform. However, cultivating and practicing the core values of contemporary Chinese socialism cannot be separated from certain social realistic resources. Besides inheriting and developing the traditional Chinese culture and values as well as the core values of Utopian socialism, the core values of capitalism are also the logical premise of cultivating and practicing the history of the core values of contemporary Chinese socialism. Moreover, the socialist core values have surpassed the historical limitations of Western values and endowed them with new connotations of socialism. The basic contents of the core values of capitalism can be summarized as freedom, equality, rule of law, human rights, fraternity, and so on.[1] Highlighting the subjective status of individuals, emphasizing the rule of law and fraternity, and advocating human rights, but at the same time, these values are progressive and hypocritical. As a socialist country, facing the current situation of great integration and collision of various ideologies and cultures in society, China treats the core values of capitalism with an open mind and adopts a dialectical scientific attitude. It affirms its progressive aspect, makes a scientific analysis of it and draws reasonable lessons from it, criticizes, surpasses, and breaks through its hypocrisy thoroughly, and endows it with a brand-new value connotation of socialism in China's social and cultural environment, thus forming the most sound socialist core values oriented to the future development direction of mankind and standing at the commanding height of human civilization. Marx and Engels' basic ideas on socialist core values are also the main ideological sources of the generation of socialist core values in our society. Marx and Engels' basic thoughts on socialist core values are mainly emancipation, freedom, equality, democracy, and so on; Lenin's basic thoughts on socialist core values are mainly: the ultimate value orientation of human's free and comprehensive development, the political values of establishing a new democratic system, the economic values of vigorously developing productive forces and the cultivation of new Communist people; Cultural values, etc. Stalin's basic thoughts on socialist core values is: common prosperity, development of productive forces, etc.

At the same time, the cultivation and practice of China's socialist core values cannot be separated from the active exploration of socialist core values by the Communist Party of China. The core values of socialism in contemporary China have been formed and developed in the great practice of socialist revolution, construction, and reform in China. They have undergone a transformation from class struggle as the core to economic construction as the center, and then to people-oriented, forming a very rich content. It is mainly embodied in Mao Zedong Thought and the theoretical system of socialism with Chinese characteristics and in a series of lines, principles, and policies of the Party. Based on these, several generations of central leading collectives of the Party, with Mao Zedong, Deng Xiaoping, Jiang Zemin, Hu Jintao, and Xi Jinping as the core, have made arduous exploration of the core

---

[1] Sun Jie. Research on the Core Values of Contemporary Chinese Socialism [D]. Party School of the Central Committee of the Communist Party of China, 2014.

socialist values from the height of the development of the times and based on the basic national conditions of China, and formed a scientific system of succession, which provides a direct theoretical source to cultivate and practice the core socialist values of contemporary China.

Promoting and cultivating the core values of contemporary Chinese socialism is the requirement of the development of the times. Its cultivation needs not only a solid mass foundation but also certain historical and realistic resources. As Marx pointed out, people always get their own ethical ideas from the actual relationship on which their class status is based. The core values of a society cannot be separated from a certain social and economic basis.[2] Therefore, cultivating and practicing the core values of contemporary Chinese socialism must also have certain social conditions. These realistic conditions come from the sound socialist market economic system, the development of the socialist democratic political system, the continuous improvement of the quality of the broad masses of the people, the competition and cooperation in the process of globalization. Therefore, on the whole, the cultivation and establishment of socialist core values in China have been tested by history and reality. It is based on the development needs of the system and society, economy and culture of the current Chinese society. It absorbs the dimensions of classical Marxist thought, contemporary Chinese Marxist thought, traditional Chinese culture thought, and Western modern civilization. The ideological dimension comes into being in four aspects.[3] Only then did we have today's 16-character policy to guide the development of all aspects of our society.

5.3   The Connotation of Socialist Core Values

"Advocating prosperity, democracy, civilization and harmony, advocating freedom, equality, justice and the rule of law, advocating patriotism, dedication, integrity and friendliness, and actively cultivating and Practicing Socialist Core values." This is our Party's new understanding of socialist core values, as well as its important contribution to cultural values and ideological and theoretical achievements. The "three advocacy" reflects the vision and demands of the state, the collective, and the individual, the high value consciousness and self-confidence of the Communist Party of China and the Chinese nation, the organic unity of the soul of rejuvenating the country, the foundation of founding the country and the foundation of strengthening the country, and the strategic decision made by the Party Central Committee based on the practice of modernization construction. On the basis of the "three advocates" of the Eighteenth National Congress, the concise and summary of the socialist core values can be summarized as follows: rule of law, justice, harmony, and happiness

---

[2] Volume 9 [M] of the anthology of Marx and Engels. Beijing: People's Publishing House, 2009:99.
[3] Wang Jie. Study on the Construction, Cultivation and Practice of Contemporary Chinese Socialist Core Values [D]. Party School of Jiangsu Provincial Committee of the Communist Party of China, 2013.

under the principle of unity of reality and objectives, state and individual, nation and the world. "Wealth and strength, democracy, civilization and harmony are the value goals at the national level. Freedom, equality, justice and the rule of law are the value orientations at the social level. Patriotism, dedication, honesty and friendliness are the values at the individual level." It regulates the core value pursuit of our country, society, and individual from three levels, reflects the common value pursuit and ideal belief of the people of all nationalities, has distinct Chinese characteristics, and constitutes a logical whole with the close connection. Richness, democracy, civilization, and harmony are the value objectives of socialist China, reflecting the inherent stipulation of socialism with Chinese characteristics at the spiritual and value levels, and reflecting the all-round value demands of socialism in politics, economy, culture, society, and ecology. Being rich and strong is the core value of socialist economic construction with Chinese characteristics. Democracy is the core value of the political construction of socialism with Chinese characteristics. Civilization is the core value of socialist cultural construction with Chinese characteristics. Harmony is the core value of socialist social and ecological construction with Chinese characteristics. Freedom, equality, justice, and the rule of law are vivid expressions of a better society, reflecting the basic requirements of Marxism, reflecting the ideal value attributes pursued unremittingly by our socialist society, and also the core values of our Party's unswerving and long-term practice. Liberty is the ultimate value of socialism. Equality is the basic premise of a socialist society. Justice is the primary value of a socialist society. The rule of law is the institutional guarantee to realize freedom, equality, and justice. Virtue, socialist morality, and the essence of Chinese Communists' revolutionary morality are also our party's new development of Marx's civic virtues and values. Patriotism is the social virtue of citizens. Professionalism is the professional ethics of citizens. Credit is the basic virtue of human beings. Friendship is a generous virtue of human kindness and tolerance.[4] Education is an important position to practice the socialist core values. Understanding the connotation of the 16-character principle of socialist core values in the field of education has long-term significance to the further implementation of ideological and political education, the cultivation and promotion of socialist core values, and to all teachers and students to be a firm believer, active disseminator, and model practitioner under the guidance of socialist core values. It is of great practical significance to effectively carry out the education of College Students' socialist core values in the dimension of morality and cultivation of human beings, to promote the all-round development of college students and to promote the great rejuvenation of the Chinese nation. In order to cultivate and Practice Socialist Core Values in the educational system, we should learn from primary school to university the virtues of building a country, a society, and a citizen. Especially for college students, they are the most promising young people, and young people are in a critical period of value formation and establishment. General Secretary Xi Jinping said that the reason why we should talk about socialist core values to young people is that the value orientation of young people determines

---

[4]Zhang Lan. The Role of Socialist Core Values in College Education [J]. New Oriental, 2018, 236 (5): 67–71.

the value orientation of the whole society in the future, and young people are in the period of forming and establishing values, so it is very important to cultivate values in this period. In this regard, General Secretary Xi Jinping also made a very vivid metaphor: "It's like buttoning when you wear clothes. If the first button is wrong, the rest of the buttons will be wrong. The buttons of life should be fastened from the beginning. 'Sinkers can dig from very shallow to very deep'." As the future builder and successor of the motherland, the contemporary youth should start from now on and from themselves, make the socialist core values become their basic adherence, form consciously pursued beliefs and concepts, make achievements in the tide of the times, and achieve their own good life.[5]

5.4   The Influence of Socialist Core Values and Its Significance to the Education and Cultivation of Adolescent Values

In China today, with the further development of the socialist market economy, great changes have taken place in all areas of society. Coupled with the impact of economic globalization, Western social trends of thought flooded into China, and people's value diversification trend became increasingly prominent. Under the social background of various ideological and cultural exchanges and collisions, the CPC Central Committee, based on reality and in the long run, clearly puts forward the cultivation and practice of socialist core values, which is of great significance for leading social trends of thought, cohesing social consensus, building spiritual home, enhancing the soft power of national culture, vigorously promoting the building of a well-off society in an all-round way, and realizing the Chinese dream of rejuvenating the Chinese nation. However, the cultivation and practice of socialist core values in contemporary China has a long way to go and still faces multiple dilemmas, which are mainly manifested in the following aspects: the loss of morality, the lack of mainstream values, the lack of value consensus, and the lack of public morality consciousness. We should carefully analyze and discuss the current dilemma of our socialist core values, and deeply analyze its causes, in order to better promote the promotion and cultivation of our socialist core values, actively guide social thoughts and values, and build a common spiritual home for the Chinese nation. As an important part of our national ideology, the socialist core value system and socialist core value play an important role in cultivating new socialist people, which put forward common values and codes of conduct for the contemporary Chinese people. To cultivate new generations of socialists and to practice the socialist core value system and socialist core values is an important issue facing the whole Party and the people. It has a very prominent social value and practical significance for the construction of a civilized, democratic, harmonious, and prosperous socialist country. Compulsory education

---

[5]Xi Jinping. Xi Jinping Talking about Governing the State [M]. Beijing: Foreign Language Publishing House, 2014:172.

and higher education are the main battlefields for systematically cultivating socialist successors. Children and adolescents are the main periods for the formation of a person's values. They can be adjusted and deepened when people enter the youth. Youth is the future of the country and the nation. Whoever wins the youth wins the future. College students are the core of youth, the pillar of the future construction and development of our country, and the builder and successor of our socialist cause. The values of college students not only affect the mainstream values of our society in the future to a great extent, but also determine the future and destiny of our country to a great extent.[6]

Since its establishment, socialist values have clearly become the positive driving force and guiding force for the development of mainstream values in our society. On March 11, 2018, the First Session of the Thirteenth National People's Congress adopted the Amendment to the Constitution of the People's Republic of China, amending "the state's public morality of advocating love for the motherland, the people, labor, science and socialism" to "the state's public morality of advocating socialist core values and advocating love for the motherland, the people, labor, science and socialism."[7] Incorporating it into the scope of the Constitution will make the orientation of socialist core values clearer. It essentially adheres to the socialist ideology of socialist core values, plays the guiding role of socialist core values in political, economic, cultural, life, and other fields, and takes the socialist core value as the leading factor in content, leads the development of other value ideas by the basic contents of socialist core values.[8]

Class culture construction and core values: class culture and individual growth
As an organization, the class plays a guiding and normative role for the individuals in the class, which cannot be separated from the construction of culture in the class. Therefore, class culture plays an important role in cultivating individual character and values. Class culture is a relatively stable combination of ideological style, emotional attitude, style of writing, mode of thinking and values shared by all members of the class. As a member of the class, students are always influenced by the class culture, which plays a normative, edifying, and assimilating role for individuals. Educational sociology holds that classes are not only a microcosm of the real society but also an organizational structure. Class culture is the soul of the class, which reflects the value orientation and behavior attitude of the class members. The construction of class culture emphasizes the positioning of class culture and the promotion of quality culture, such as class value pursuit, goal, code of conduct and quality improvement, which lays the keynote for class style of study and class atmosphere, guides the direction of students' professional learning and amateur activities, and is the core issue for

---

[6]Research and Practice of Class Culture Construction in Primary Schools Based on Socialist Core Values [D]. Guangxi Normal University, 2016.

[7]Qiushi. The Important Characteristics of the 2018 Amendment to the Constitution[EB/OL]. (2018-03-12) [2019-05-29]. http://www.qstheory.cn/wp/2018-03/12/c_1122526920.htm.

[8]Jiang Cuiting. A Study on the Dominance of Socialist Core Values [D]. Shanghai Normal University, 2018.

class members to gain a sense of belonging and honor.[9] In the class, collectivism is more valuable than individual demands and values, and the construction of class culture plays a direct role in promoting individual participation in collective activities in terms of behavior, thought, and emotion. The longest education an individual receives in the process of growing up is school education, and the most lasting education is the recessive education brought about by class culture. Especially in the stage of compulsory education, class culture has positive significance for shaping individual character and behavior. The development of individual morality and values runs through the whole learning period, and the moral education of individual students also runs through all periods of individual learning. Whether it is the ideological and political education work in colleges or the moral education work in the compulsory education stage, it is an important to grasp to realize "building up morality and cultivating people" in the field of education. At present, moral education and value cultivation of individual students in our education system are mainly implemented through class education. A good class culture construction in class education has an important influence on class construction and the development of students' personality. Therefore, the head teacher should fully realize that in class collective construction, we should use various effective resources to create the important value of class culture, pay attention to the overall design of class culture construction, and give full play to the educational function of class culture. In order to have a good class culture in a class, we must put moral education in the first place. Targeting moral education as the training objective of class culture construction mainly depends on educators, mainly class teachers. According to the social requirements and the individual needs of students and the characteristics and laws of physical and mental development, class teachers provide positive guidance to students purposefully, systematically, and step by step, and then further enable students to actively accept education, thus forming good ideological and moral character. This requires that the construction of class culture can infiltrate individual values education from all levels, and be stratified according to the organizational structure, including four aspects: class spiritual culture, class material culture, class system culture, and class behavior culture. Class spiritual culture, which is the inherent mechanism of class culture, includes class rules and regulations, disciplinary norms, class rituals, and so on. For example, to establish detailed class and group activity records, discipline system, leave system, management system, tutor system, award evaluation system, dormitory health system, etc., not only to ensure the orderly class but also to enable students to develop a sense of system and rules before entering society.

Class behavior culture pays attention to class values, moral compliance, taste needs, and so on, which exerts a subtle influence on students. Under the influence of the class environment, students' speech and behavior, interpersonal communication, and behavioral ability will be improved and developed together, thus realizing

---

[9]Xu Lanying, Liu I. Research on the Integration of Socialist Core Values into the Construction of Class Culture in Universities: Based on the Analysis of Excellent Class Collections at the Provincial Level of Hebei University [J]. Journal of the College of Adult Education, Hebei University, 2019, 21 (1): 108–112.

the essential transformation from restraint to consciousness. Class material culture has the characteristics of visible, concretization, and visualization. For example, the construction of class environment, the improvement of facilities, the design of landscape, the management of books, the class emblem, class flag, class uniform, class publications, website construction, etc., which condense the collective wisdom of students. Class hard culture can not only enhance students' sense of belonging and participation, enhance class cohesion, but also stimulate students' imagination and creativity. Class system construction not only pays attention to standardization but also pays attention to the guiding role of values in system construction. In the construction of class system, such as class daily management system, reward and punishment system, class committee management system and so on, the content of socialist core values is integrated, and students are helped to develop the ideological concepts and behavioral habits consistent with the requirements of socialist core values. A collective with good habits is bound to be a collective with the same goal. Only by forming a good class culture can the students in the class be bound and driven. That is to say, using group pressure directly affects every student in the collective, making them feel pressure, and then ensuring that each member in learning, life, discipline, etc., not only comply with the requirements of collective interests, but also have a positive impact on the formation of good personal habits. In the school environment, the development of individuals can not be separated from the construction of class culture. The construction of class culture is a long-term and systematic project, including class spiritual culture, class material culture, class system culture and class behavior culture. At the same time, schools are also the main position for the education of socialist core values., relying on class culture can better deepen the concept of values education and enhance its influence. In order to achieve this educational function goal, it is necessary to establish effective educational strategies in practice in order to better promote the long-term development of education.

Students' individual growth and socialist core values

As a growing individual, students need to establish correct values. In May 2018, General Secretary Xi Jinping put forward four hopes to the young people during his visit to Peking University. He asked them to "be loyal to the motherland and the people", "be ambitious and strive for success", "be true in knowledge and skills", "be a combination of knowledge and practice and a doer", and should shoulder the mission of socialist builders and successors and strive for building a well-off society in an all-round way and building a strong socialist modernization country in an all-round way. To conscientiously study and comprehensively implement the spirit of the Nineteenth National Congress of the Party and deeply understand the ardent hope put forward by General Secretary Xi Jinping for the youth, It is necessary to make it an important historical task for us to establish morality and cultivate people and cultivate new people of the times in the current and future educational front. Therefore, we must give full play to the role of socialist core values. We believe that the core values of socialism involving the state, society and individuals have a common orientation, that is, to establish morality, to establish the morality of the state, to establish the morality of the society and to establish the morality of the citizens. To cultivate and practice socialist core values in colleges and universities, the key is to establish morality and cultivate people from the above three aspects.

The cultivation of students' socialist core values is not only conducive to the healthy growth of students, but also the need to practice Marxist educational theory.[10] Practice has proved that Marxist educational theory conforms to the development of our country and meets the needs of society. Socialist core values are the essential requirements of socialist ideology. In the new era, China is in the stage of great development, adjustment and transformation. People's ideology is gradually diversified, and their values are also complex and turbulent. For college students, on the one hand, they are being infiltrated by western ideology and culture. By means of academic discussions, visits and exchanges, they infiltrate the "Westernization" ideology into college students, which has seriously affected their psychology and threatened their national consciousness and spirit. On the other hand, the development of the information age has made the problem of information pollution more and more serious, students will inevitably be infringed by polluted information in the process of contacting the Internet and mobile phones, which will destroy their world outlook, outlook on life, values and moral concepts.[11] Therefore, it is of far-reaching practical significance to actively practice Marxist educational theory, adhere to the fundamental task of cultivating people by virtue, strengthen the education of socialist core values of contemporary college students and safeguard ideological security. The cultivation of students' values is also the need to train future socialist builders and successors. The socialist core values are not only the inheritance of the excellent tradition of the Chinese nation, but also the need of social development in the new era. Socialist core values are the value standards of social moral judgment, the profound embodiment of the state and national cultural consciousness and theoretical consciousness and can purify the social atmosphere and cultivate civilized fashion. Socialist core values play a vital role in building a strong socialist cultural country and improving the country's cultural soft power. Nowadays, China's social development has entered a critical period, inevitably encountering many difficulties. It is imperative to call on social forces and improve social cohesion. College students are a new force in the development of socialist modernization in the new era. Therefore, it is necessary to strengthen the education of college students' socialist core values, cultivate their sense of responsibility and mission, strengthen their ideals and beliefs, help them to study scientific and cultural knowledge, improve their innovative and creative abilities, and guide them to consciously devote themselves to the construction of socialism with Chinese characteristics. The cultivation of students' values is also the need to promote students' all-round development. The main goal of contemporary college students' education is to enhance students' ability to value judgment and choice, cultivate good moral customs and moral consciousness, guide students to establish lofty ideals and social responsibility, and train talents with both moral and talent

[10]Chen Huawen. Research on the Education of College Students' Socialist Core Values from the Perspective of Lide Shuren [D]. 2016.

[11]Zheng Zehui. On the Innovation of Community Police Work under the Informationization Conditions [J]. Guangdong Public Security Science and Technology, 2014, 22 (1): 8–12.

and comprehensive development. Therefore, colleges and universities must adhere to the educational concept of building morality and cultivating people, constantly strengthen the education of socialist core values, pay attention to the construction of science and culture, at the same time, cultivate students' good moral quality and comprehensive quality, so that students can actively participate in socialist construction, constantly improve themselves and achieve all-round development.[12]

The relationship between class culture and socialist core values

The socialist core values are the highest embodiment of the pursuit of the spiritual values of the state and the nation. The construction of class culture based on socialist core values is the construction of class spiritual culture. Spirit refers to a person's spiritual outlook through his words and deeds and a kind of consciousness through his thinking. Only when a person has a spirit he can be energetic. Similarly, the class spirit of a class is a kind of collective spirit and collective concept that the members of the class show in class activities. Class spirit is embodied in class members' organizational discipline, action efficiency, learning enthusiasm, harmonious relationship between teachers and students and classmates, etc. Positive and healthy class spiritual culture is the source of vigor and vitality of the class, a powerful driving force for the healthy development of the class, and a powerful influence to promote the healthy growth of the class students. She is like an invisible big hand, pushing every member of the class to make continuous efforts toward the collective common behavior goals and thinking direction, playing the role of "promoting righteousness and dispelling evil" for the collective, helping the class to form a spirit of unity, friendship, and upward struggle. Class spiritual culture refers to the class group spirit formed under the guidance of the head teacher and the participation of the whole class, including class ideal, class goal, class spirit, class style of study, etc. To integrate socialist core values into the spiritual and cultural construction of college classes, first of all, to establish class ideals and class objectives that meet the requirements of socialist core values, to integrate the content of socialist core values into class spiritual culture, and strive to be a civilized class group and an excellent class group. Secondly, some cultural symbols, such as class motto, class song, class emblem, and class uniform, are designed to embody the core values of socialism, so that students can be influenced and educated by the core values of socialism imperceptibly. Finally, under the guidance of socialist core values, we should strengthen the construction of class style and style of study, guide students to form the habit of loving learning and thinking, and let students be influenced and nurtured subtly in a good class atmosphere.

Class culture is the sum of the thinking mode, moral norms, behavior habits, and values, which are gradually formed through the interaction between teachers and students in the long-term practical activities of the class, embodying the characteristics of the class and which are unanimously agreed by the classmates. It mainly includes class spiritual culture, material culture, system culture, behavior culture, and so on.

---

[12]Yu Xin. Research on the Education of College Students' Socialist Core Values under the Dimension of Lide Shuren[J]. Journal of Jiangxi Electric Power Vocational and Technical College, 2018, 31(12): 160–161+168.

The socialist core values are the latest theoretical achievements put forward by our Party in the face of the new situation, and deepen our understanding of the essence of socialism and its core values. Socialist core values and class culture in colleges and universities belong to the socialist culture with Chinese characteristics. They complement each other, promote each other, and are dialectically unified. On the one hand, socialist core values are the inherent requirements of class culture in colleges and universities, and the construction of class culture in colleges and universities should be guided by socialist core values. On the other hand, class culture in colleges and universities is an important platform for the construction of socialist core values, through which the education of socialist core values can be implemented.[13] Classroom culture with Chinese characteristics is the embodiment of socialist core values. Class culture is to cultivate morality, and socialist core values are also to cultivate morality. Class culture is a way of practice and cultivation, and values are spiritual guidance.

Socialist core values lay a theoretical foundation for the construction of class culture

Socialist core values are the mainstream values in today's society. It reflects a universal value pursuit and value orientation from the national leadership to the common people in the current era. It plays a very important leading role in people's ideological, life value orientation, and moral concepts. On October 18, 2017, General Secretary Xi Jinping pointed out in the report of the Nineteenth National Congress that "we should integrate socialist core values into all aspects of social development and transform them into people's emotional identity and behavior habits." Cultivating and practicing core values runs through the whole process of education and is the core content of building morality and cultivating people in colleges and universities.[14] On January 17, 2014, People's Daily published a commentator's article "Integrating Core Values into the Whole Process of National Education - On How to Cultivate and Practice Socialist Core Values." The article says: when we cultivate socialist core values, we should not only pay attention to basic education but also extend socialist core values to higher education, adult education, vocational and technical education, and other fields.[15] The core values provide theoretical guidance and ideological guidance for the school education of all levels and all kinds of education systems. Therefore, "core values" is the ideological basis of class culture construction. Ideological guidance is fundamental, which not only determines the direction of class cultural construction but also determines the spiritual outlook of class members. "Opinions of the

---

[13]Liu Yu. The path of integrating socialist core values into the construction of class culture in Colleges and universities [J].Quality Education in West China, 2019, 5(5): 37–39.

[14]Xi Jinping. Winning the Great Victory of Socialism with Chinese Characteristics in the New Era by Building a Well-off Society in an All-round Way—Report at the Nineteenth National Congress of the Communist Party of China [EB/OL]. http://www.xinhuanet.com/2017-10/27/c_1121867529.htm.

[15]Commentator of People's Daily. Integrating Core Values into the Whole Process of National Education—On How to Cultivate and Practice Socialist Core Values [N]. People's Daily, 2014-01-17 (01).

Central Committee of the Communist Youth League of the Ministry of Education on Strengthening and Improving the Construction of Campus Culture in Colleges and Universities" points out that we should always adhere to the correct political standpoint and take the socialist core values as the basis, guide college students to form diligent learning, moral cultivation, clear discrimination, and solid individual inner self-cultivation, and construct social public spirit such as patriotism and social conscience.[16] "Core Values" closely combines the construction of class cultural connotation, the ideological guidance of students and the national construction and the cultivation of national spirit, cultivates teachers' and students' morality, beautifies the campus humanistic environment, and leads the social fashion. "Core values" put forward value objectives from different levels, which are the "beacons" of all social activities, contain the connotation and essence of our excellent traditional culture, and are the positive energy of personal development, social progress, and national prosperity. The important mission of class culture construction is to promote people's all-round development and play a leading and exemplary role in school class culture construction. The "core values" accurately answer the practical education questions such as what kind of people to educate and how to educate people. It is a yardstick to measure the concept of school education. Therefore, the construction of class culture is in line with the "core values" of the goal pursuit and value realization.

Primary education is to train people who meet the needs of social construction and development. The construction of primary school class culture should always be based on socialist core values, combine core values of education with the concrete reality of students' learning and growth, guide students to set up lofty ideals from childhood, study hard, and strive to make them become a new generation with social responsibility, innovative spirit, and practical ability, serving the motherland and the people in the future, fighting for the cause of communism all one's life.

The socialist core values provide the correct direction for the construction of class culture

Class culture construction meets the requirements of "core values", and socialist core values provide the direction of value education for class culture construction. Values reflect people's judgments and views on things. Core values show value pursuit from three levels: state, society, and individuals. It also puts forward construction requirements for every citizen and collective, which is everyone's code of conduct and value orientation. The school undertakes the important mission of cultivating "core values" and applies it to the whole process of teaching, management, and service. Class collective, as the "foundation" education carrier of school, undertakes the basic work of shaping class image, creating a school cultural atmosphere, and cultivating students' values. It is an important platform for students to cultivate their socialized values. Among them, the orientation of class culture, value pursuit, and individual feelings directly affect students' recognition of "core values". Therefore, the construction of

---

[16]Central Committee of the Communist Youth League, Ministry of Education. Opinions on Strengthening and Improving Campus Culture Construction in Colleges and Universities [EB/OL].http://old.moe.gov.cn//publicfiles/business/htmlfiles/moe/moe_512/200504/6653.html.

class culture must conform to the connotation and value orientation of "core values". Today's society is an Information Age with ever-changing information. The impact of reform and opening-up on people's thinking and the communication convenience brought by the Internet have changed people's way of thinking tremendously. The complex and changeable social environment and the constant impact of multiculturalism make people's way of life, moral standards, and value pursuit constantly change. Primary school students are in the enlightenment period of outlook on life and values. They are easy to accept new things but lack the ability to distinguish right from wrong. Their personality quality has greater plasticity but is vulnerable to external influence. Complex social environment, especially the impact of the network on the physical and mental development of primary school students has a tremendous impact. It is not uncommon for students to surf the Internet and become addicted to online games. In the construction of class culture, how to grasp the profound influence of the complex changes of social environment on pupils' psychology and behavior, and how to promote the development of students' healthy personality, it is urgent for teachers to find a correct value to guide students strongly. Socialist core values, as a value orientation generally followed by a country and all the people, have such a powerful force, which can point out the right direction for the construction of class culture, and help teachers to educate students to be positive in the construction of class culture, distinguish right from wrong, and grow healthy.

Socialist core values put forward requirements for individual citizenship, and the cultivation of these qualities needs to be realized by means of activities and systems that contain socialist core values in organizations and cultures. In fact, the establishment of socialist core values provides work direction and educational objectives for the construction of class culture in schools at all levels. Constructing class spirit centered on core values, creating a material environment reflecting core values, forming rules and regulations based on core values, and carrying out behavior activities guided by core values. Socialist core values are the moral norms, ideological character, and value orientation generally recognized and widely accepted by the whole country and nation. In 2014, the document of the Party Group of the Ministry of Education of the Communist Party of China in 2014, "The Opinions of the Central Committee of the Communist Youth League on Promoting the Construction of Long-term Mechanism of Cultivating and Practicing Socialist Core Values in Schools of All Levels and Various Types" further established that the socialist core values are the important judgments made by our Party in cohesion with the consensus of the values of the whole Party and the whole society. Actively cultivating and practicing socialist core values is the core requirement for schools to implement the fundamental task of Building Morality and cultivating people. Socialist core values involve three levels: state, society, and individual. They all have a common orientation, that is, to establish morality of the state, society, and citizens. To cultivate and Practice Socialist Core Values in Colleges and universities, the key is to cultivate morality and cultivate people from the above three aspects. The purpose of education is to cultivate people by virtue. As an important part of moral education in schools, the construction of class culture must be consistent with the educational policy and objectives of the state. The content of socialist core values should be refined and materialized into educational and teaching activities, and students' healthy personality and overall quality development should be devoted to. Therefore, in carrying out the cultural construction of primary school classes, we should take the socialist core values as the guide, formulate the objectives of class cultural construction and educational objectives: On the one hand, students are trained in morality through emotional and will training, and on the other hand, students are inspired by knowledge imparting. We should take the promotion of patriotism as the core, the education of national feelings, social care, and personality cultivation as the focus, and improve students' moral character and personality cultivation. In the construction of class culture, we should rely on the construction of material environment, carry out ecological civilization education to students, and guide them to establish the consciousness of protecting the environment and protecting nature. We should take class activities as a way to guide students to handle interpersonal relationships correctly, be kind, respect others, love and harmony; guide students to distinguish right from wrong, abide by discipline and law, and develop good habits of behavior through the construction of a good class system; and guide students to cultivate self-cultivation, good moral character based on traditional cultural education.[17]

The socialist core values provide the content basis for the development of individual values in class culture

Class culture is to cultivate morality, and socialist core values are also to cultivate morality. Class culture is the practice and cultivation of mainstream values, and socialist values are the spiritual guide of individual development. The core values belong to the category of civic literacy education, and students are successors of socialist construction. Students can learn and establish values through the influence of long-term class culture. Only after entering the society can we become a modern citizen with ideal, culture, morality, and pursuit. Socialist core values provide guidance for the construction of class culture. Socialist core values provide top-level design for the construction of class culture. Class culture construction influences and guides individuals through specific systems, environment, and behavioral activities, and cultivates and nurtures citizens' qualities needed by future society through specific details. In order to deepen the 16-character principle of socialist core values in character education and value education, the process of students' individual acceptance of education is the process of establishing and internalizing these qualities and values. Comrade Xi Jinping once emphasized that in order to cultivate and Practice Socialist Core values, we should start from dolls, schools, textbooks, classrooms, and minds, so as to internalize socialist core values into people's spiritual pursuit.[18] Socialist core values education is the primary content of moral education in schools. It lays the foundation for students to learn to recognize, to learn to behave, to learn to do things, and to learn to survive. Class culture construction is to adopt a lively

---

[17]Liu Qiong. Research and Practice of Class Culture Construction in Primary School Based on Socialist Core Values [D]. 2016.

[18]Xi Jinping. Fostering and promoting socialist core values as the basic project of cohesion, cohesion and strength [Eb/OL]. http://theory.people.com.cn/n/2014/0226/c239645-24467754.html.

way that students like to hear and see,through carrying out rich and colorful class activities with vivid content and novel forms, it closely links students' life and social reality, guides students to start from side to side and from small things, permeates the contents of socialist core values into students' minds, and enables them to realize socialist core in practice.

To infiltrate the socialist core values in the construction of class culture, first of all, to ensure that the core values should adapt to the physical and mental characteristics of young people and the law of growth, and in the process of propaganda and learning, first of all, to strengthen students' understanding of the core values. Combining the basic requirements of socialist core values, developing class culture construction activities.[19] For example, the construction of class culture wall, around the socialist core values to build class culture wall, create a lively and innovative learning environment, while deepening students' understanding of the socialist core values. We can also collect articles around the socialist core values, choose a few words in the socialist core values "24 words" to express our understanding, with unlimited subjects, select representative excellent articles for class members to learn, strengthen the understanding of socialist core values, and build a harmonious, friendly, and mutually supportive class atmosphere. We should improve class rules and regulations, implement reward and punishment policies, standardize classroom order and enhance the learning atmosphere. A harmonious and quiet learning atmosphere plays a positive role in students' learning, thinking, words, and deeds. The construction of class culture also requires the cultivation of collective consciousness, the organization of students to carry out collective outward-bound training, and the combination of socialist core values education to convey the essence of students' outward-bound training. Setting up a collective consciousness, although students are an individual, the classes composed of many members become a collective. Many classes form a class collective. Only when these classes are united, can schools be established. Therefore, we should have a collective consciousness. Words and deeds not only represent individuals, but also classes representing our own schools.

Deeply study Lei Feng's spirit. "Lei Feng Spirit is eternal and vivid reflection of socialist core values." We should carry out various forms of learning Lei Feng practice activities, integrate Lei Feng Spirit into life and normalize Lei Feng's behavior, not just in the short 30 days of "Lei Feng Moon". Focusing on urban and rural communities, with mutual care and social service as the main purpose, we will help the needy people, including empty-nesters, left-behind children, laid-off workers, disabled people, and other disadvantaged groups. Encourage students to learn Lei Feng, start from small things, start from what they can do, and carry out voluntary assistance activities. "Core Values" has rich connotations and embodies the excellent Chinese traditional culture and Chinese spirit. It has a long history of cultural accumulation and development space. It can not only inject cultural resources and cultural power into the class but also give full play to the advantages of important festivals and traditional festivals in disseminating the mainstream values of society.

---

[19] Ren Junzhan. Exploring the Effective Infiltration of Socialist Core Values in the Construction of Class Culture [J]. Modern Communication, 2017 (13): 146–147.

Before traditional holidays or statutory holidays begin, it can convey the significance and origin of students' festivals. For example, before the founding of the Party and National Day, we should strengthen the promotion of revolutionary spirit, carry forward the excellent traditions formed in the process of revolution, construction, and reform, and carry forward the national spirit and the spirit of the times. Before the Spring Festival, Mid-Autumn Festival, and other festivals, students are guided to feel the feelings of homesickness and family reunion contained in such festivals. We should seize the current events and disasters that have occurred recently, pay attention to the state's handling methods in dealing with emergencies, and use educational models to carry out various educational activities. We should strengthen the construction of educational bases for patriotism and publicize and promote patriotism from online to offline. We should constantly improve the education of excellent traditional Chinese culture, form an effective form and long-term mechanism for activities of loving learning, working, and motherland, and strive to train socialist builders and successors with all-round development of morality, intelligence, physical fitness, and beauty.

We should give full play to the "four links and five plates" to promote the socialist cultural values in the construction of class culture. Combining cultural education with skill training, and guided by socialist core values, we can cultivate a class culture with high comprehensive quality and ideological and moral level as well as comprehensive talents. For example, the five major sections of the project, poetry contest, classical morning reading, reading sharing, youth and etiquette learning and training, improve students' learning ability and cultural level from various aspects, and enhance the connotation of socialist core values. The "Four Rings" includes four links, including establishing rules and regulations, conducting a series of lectures, conducting speech competitions and social practice activities. Establish rules and regulations, from the school point of view require students to learn and self-restraint, improve the construction of spiritual civilization in class culture; To carry out a series of lectures, including the ideas conveyed by the lecturer to the students and the communication between the students and the lecturer, enrich the students' thoughts in the communication; Speech competitions and social practice require students to deepen their understanding. The study of socialist core values and the construction of class culture should not stop at theoretical study but should go deeper into practice and learn from practice.

Chapter 6
Classroom Culture and Chinese Traditional Culture: Concept and Practice

This chapter involves examining the relationship between classroom culture and Chinese traditional culture contextually. Introduction of classroom culture, The overview of campus culture, research Contents of campus culture in China, review of Chinese studies on campus culture in the Chinese context, the relationship between class culture and campus culture, and case studies on the relationship between class culture and campus culture all concentrate on figuring how to examine the relations between classroom culture and Chinese traditional culture, specifically.

6.1 Introduction of Classroom Culture

Class culture can be called group culture. Class culture should be a combination of common beliefs, common values, and common attitudes of class groups. The construction of class culture refers to the process in which class members (including teachers and students) purposefully and systematically create material and spiritual wealth that meets the requirements of social development and their own development needs in practical activities.

With the further deepening of the new curriculum reform, the attention to the construction of class culture has been continuously raised. Many teachers are aware of the importance of creating a good class culture atmosphere for the growth of student groups. However, due to various reasons, the construction of class culture still shows many problems to be solved in the development of the past decade, such as the uniqueness of the main body of class culture construction; Cultural construction is too formal; class cultural construction lacks systematic planning; class material culture lags behind; class cultural construction lacks the cultivation of creativity; class cultural construction lacks theoretical support; insufficient attention is paid to student case consultation and counseling; class cultural personality is lacking.

© Springer Nature Singapore Pte Ltd. 2020
X. Zhu and J. Li, *Classroom Culture in China*, Perspectives on Rethinking and Reforming Education, https://doi.org/10.1007/978-981-15-1827-0_6

At present, the study of class culture also shows some characteristics: increasing attention; expanding the scope of research objects; gradual refinement of research areas; integration of multiple research models, and so on.

6.2 The Overview of Campus Culture

6.2.1 Connotation and Composition of Campus Culture

Different researchers have different views on the connotation of campus culture. Lin Qingjiang, a Taiwanese scholar, defines campus culture as "the value and behavior system constituted by the constituents of the school is called campus culture" in his New Theory of Educational Sociology. He also holds that there are six factors contributing to the formation of campus culture: teacher culture, student culture, school administrator culture, school-related community culture, school material culture, school traditions, rituals and its rules, and regulations.[1] Zhu Yanjie wrote a special chapter "Shaping campus culture: A Survival Strategy" in his School Management Theory, which discussed the problem of campus culture. He defines campus culture as "the so-called campus culture refers to the sum of values, codes of conduct and common style formed within a school and followed and assimilated by its members."[2] Qin Zaidong believes that campus culture is a closed and self-circulating "gravitational system", whose tension is influenced by the comprehensive force of school soul, school regulations, and school appearance, especially the influence of spiritual form; campus culture is a spiritual climate or atmosphere in the campus which takes values as the core and embodies the activity form and material form of carrying this value system. On the one hand, campus culture is the accumulation of school historical tradition, on the other hand, it is the reflection of social culture on the campus. Campus culture is essentially a community culture. Campus culture belongs to social ideology in its nature, and its function is ultimately the political, moral, and psychological impact of an ideological or spiritual factor on campus people.[3] Gao Zhanxiang, Shi Huanan, and others define campus culture as a group culture with students as the main body, campus as the main space and campus spirit as the main characteristics. It is all material and spiritual achievements created by all teachers and students.[4]

Scholars in China define campus culture mainly from three perspectives[5]: (1) campus culture is an organizational culture, which is the sum of all the existing ways of school organization, including the material and spiritual culture of the school;

---

[1] Lin Qingjiang. A New View on Educational Sociology [M]. Taiwan: Taipei Wunan Book Publishing Company, 1981.

[2] Zhu Yanjie. School Management Theory [M]. Shenyang: Liaoning Education Press, 1988.

[3] Xie (2006).

[4] Fan (2014).

[5] See footnote 4.

(2) campus culture is the spiritual wealth, cultural atmosphere created and formed by teachers and students through educational activities, and the activity form and material form that carries these spiritual wealth and cultural atmosphere; (3) campus culture is a complex form of values and behavioral attitudes of all activities in the school, including the standards, attitudes, beliefs, behaviors, values, rituals, traditions, and so on followed and assimilated by members.

In conclusion, this study tends to define campus culture as a subculture of society, which is a unique cultural form formed consciously or unconsciously in the process of school development. Campus culture can be subdivided into material culture, system culture, spiritual culture, and curriculum activity culture. The material culture of the campus includes the campus environment, educational places, equipment, and facilities, the organizational system culture includes the level and form of the organization, rules and regulations, role norms, etc. School spiritual culture is the core of campus culture. Spiritual culture has cognitive components, such as school group composition and individual understanding of educational purposes, process and rules; emotional components such as school members' attachment, identification and love to schools, teachers and students, and their sense of responsibility, belonging, and superiority in schools, which are typical manifestations of positive emotions; value components, such as the value orientation that schools adore together; ideal components, such as the goals expressed in school mottos and school songs. The interaction of these factors will form the unique campus style of a school. Campus culture affects the direction and mode of school running, and it will permeate into the spirit and behavior of every school member. Forming a good and unique campus culture is of great significance to running a school well.[6]

6.2.2   Composition of Campus Culture

For the composition of campus culture, there are "dichotomy", "trichotomy", and "quarterly" viewpoints. Wang Dinghua believes that campus culture can be divided into the ideological culture and specific culture. Liu Zujun divides campus culture into substantive culture, institutional culture, and conceptual culture. Gu Mingyuan believes that campus culture includes spiritual culture, institutional culture, and campus material culture, and its core values. Zheng Jinzhou believes that the three main types of campus culture are teacher culture, student culture, and curriculum culture. Zhao Zhongjian divides campus culture into spiritual culture, institutional culture, action culture, and material culture.[7]

---

[6]See footnote 3.
[7]See footnote 4.

6.3   Research Contents of Campus Culture in China

6.3.1   Characteristics of Campus Culture

Researchers believe that the characteristics of campus culture are mainly reflected in the following aspects[8,9]:

Campus culture is independent
The independence of campus culture is not only embodied in the subject, environment, mode of cultural creation, and the means of recording cultural achievements, but also in the process of communication with social culture or other subcultural systems. It is this independence that makes campus culture self-contained and has its own unique form, evolution and inheritance rules, as well as its own way of existence and historical origin.

Campus culture has distinct educational and normative characteristics
Schools are places for purposeful and planned training of talents. It must train and educate students according to the requirements of social progress, which determines the educational nature of campus culture. The difference between campus culture and other cultural forms in education is mainly manifested in the fact that the educational nature of campus culture is conscious and has a clear purpose.

Campus culture is selective
campus culture is an open culture. It contacts all kinds of cultures at home and abroad by imparting knowledge and developing science. It must critically inherit and selectively absorb the social values, knowledge system, moral standards, and behavioral patterns of the past and present, thus forming its own unique cultural system.

Campus culture is at the forefront of social culture
Compared with other community cultures, it has a certain advance. This feature is based on the following two reasons: on the one hand, because campus culture is a high-level culture, the cultural people in high-level culture are generally active in thinking, dare to change, dare to pioneer, walk in the forefront of the times, and play a model leading role in society; on the other hand, most of the school cultural people are young students, who dare to act bravely and are full of criticism. The social culture itself has contradictions and conflicts, that is, relatively stable and constantly changing. Young students are in the forefront of this contradiction and conflict.

---

[8]Mao (2008).
[9]See footnote 3.

Campus culture is characterized by extensive participation
The broad scope of campus culture is all-round. From the perspective of the main body of campus culture, it includes not only various kinds of rich and colorful specific activities, but also deeper education methods such as teaching, management, service, environment, and culture. From the content, it includes not only the construction of spiritual culture, but also material cultures such as campus layout facilities, rules, and regulations.

Campus culture has independence and diversity
Because of its specific subject, environment, mode of cultural creation and the unique means of recording cultural achievements, campus culture can influence social culture and other subcultural systems with its distinct personality and form its own system. It has its own unique rules of formation, evolution, inheritance, and dissemination, and its own way of existence and historical traceability. The construction of colorful campus culture is not only beautiful scenery but also a three-dimensional and attractive textbook.

Campus culture has distinct characteristics of the times
Different historical periods and different historical stages of social development can reflect the highlights of the times in campus culture. Schools have a group of people who have more knowledge, and are also at the forefront of information dissemination, which has a certain degree of advance. Therefore, school moral educators will inevitably use and control the characteristics of campus culture to cultivate talents that meet the requirements of the development of the times.

6.3.2   Functions of Campus Culture

Campus culture plays an important role in school moral education, which is determined by its own function. Campus culture has many functions, such as guidance function, cohesion function, coordination function, incentive function, control function, assimilation function, radiation function, and so on. Its main manifestations are as follows:

Campus culture has a clear guiding function. Campus culture can integrate the thoughts and behaviors of all teachers and students into the development goals and personnel training objectives of the school, ensure the direction of school development, reflect the spirit of the school, and gradually form a suitable environment and atmosphere.

Campus culture has a strong cohesive function. The campus culture contains the common values, ideals, beliefs, behavioral norms, and other group consciousness recognized by all teachers and students. It is a kind of spiritual adhesive, which can make teachers and students have a sense of belonging, enhance cohesion and centripetal force.

Campus culture has a remarkable coordinating function. The common ideals and goals and common codes of conduct contained in campus culture, which are recognized by all teachers and students, closely link teachers, management cadres, service personnel, and students. So that they can easily communicate with each other, and can coordinate interpersonal relationships within the school so that the whole school can operate harmoniously.

Campus culture has an intrinsic incentive function. Campus culture emphasizes respect, relationship, cultivation, and improvement of teachers and students, pays attention to meeting the high-level spiritual needs of teachers and students, and actively plays the main role of teachers and students in school construction. School moral education is to maximize the enthusiasm, initiative, and creativity of teachers, staff and students in learning and work, in order to achieve the established educational goals.

6.3.3 Construction of Campus Culture

In view of the construction of campus culture, the researchers mainly focus on the problems existing in the current construction of campus culture in China and the corresponding countermeasures.

On the one hand, there are some problems and drawbacks that can not be ignored in the construction of campus culture, which affect the healthy development of campus culture and needs to be seriously rethought. Some scholars believe that there is a problem of "five weights and five lightnesses" in the current campus culture construction. First, emphasis should be laid on externalization rather than internalization; second, emphasis should be laid on hardening rather than softening; third, emphasis should be laid on change rather than evolution; fourth, emphasis should be laid on strengthening and lightening influence; finally, emphasis should be laid on materialization rather than humanization.[10] Mao Lifen believes that the main problems in the construction of campus culture are as follows: First, the construction of campus culture is facing fierce conflicts of various cultures. The first is the conflict between traditional culture and modern culture, the second is the conflict between Eastern culture and Western culture, and the third is the conflict between material civilization and spiritual civilization. In contemporary China, because the socialist market economy is still in the process of construction, which is not yet mature and perfect, there is still a big gap between the level of economic development and that of the Western developed countries. In practice, the tendency of simply paying attention to economic construction and neglecting spiritual shaping is quite serious. Second, network culture has a huge impact on traditional campus culture. Network culture is also true and false, leading to some students may escape reality and replace

---

[10]See footnote 4.

reality with illusion. Immediate and fast network culture makes people's thinking mode and level narrow and shallow, and weakens people's thinking and exploration of deep-seated problems. The interconnection and interaction of network culture make a small number of young college students expand their self-consciousness and individualism, get used to aimless living conditions, and create a life attitude of game life.[11] In addition, the researcher combines his own experience in running a school and summarizes the problems existing in the construction of campus culture as follows[12]:

Focus on investment and neglect management and utilization
In recent years, with the attention and support of the state and society, the hardware resources of most schools have been greatly improved. Especially some primary and secondary schools in urban areas have invested a lot of money in the construction of school hardware and software, and built high-grade computer rooms, multimedia classrooms, libraries, reading rooms, etc. But the effect of these teaching resources in actual use is far from the original blueprint. The main reason is that some of the equipment is flashy and unrealistic, and the management system is not practical. In view of this problem, school leaders and teachers should strengthen their understanding of teaching resources and teaching functions, attach importance to them ideologically, improve management level, improve resource management and use system, and make precious resources an effective campus culture. Schools should give full play to their advantages in running schools, talents, culture, and civilization, and open their sports venues, cultural and entertainment facilities, libraries, and laboratories to the community. Schools can establish extensive contacts with enterprises, scientific research institutions and cultural groups, strengthen the positive interaction and cooperation between schools and communities, enhance the influence and radiation of the community, and promote the material and spiritual cultural construction of the community.

Focusing on the form of activities, ignoring the content and process
School cultural activities, a kind of behavioral culture, are the dynamic manifestation of campus culture. Therefore, through various cultural recreational activities, including teaching in the form of beauty and pleasure, increasing knowledge, cultivating sentiment, improving physique, cultivating a collectivism spirit, perfecting personality and promoting students' all-round development, it is certainly beneficial to the construction of campus culture. However, school cultural activities are only a carrier. Through activities, one kind of value should be strengthened. The core issue of campus culture is the establishment of school group values, which are recognized by all teachers and students. It exists in every specific behavior and relationship between teachers and students in the whole school, and embodies the general prin-

---

[11] See footnote 8.
[12] See footnote 3.

ciples, attitudes, will, performance, and behavior habits of teachers and students in dealing with things. However, in many school activities, due to the neglect of the organizers of the process of activities and the effectiveness of education, the effect of activities is difficult to achieve the best.

Pay attention to the unity of the school as a whole and ignore the cultural characteristics of the class.

From the point of view of cultural ecology, the class is a cultural and ecological organization composed of teachers and many students with different family culture backgrounds, different community culture backgrounds, different personalities, and different temperaments. Classrooms are places where classes teach, and students learn by themselves. Students spend 75% of their time in the classroom. The classroom constitutes a "cultural ecosphere". The advantages and disadvantages of the "cultural ecosphere" in this ecosphere directly affect the physical and mental health of teachers and students and the effect of education. Just as everyone has his own personality characteristics, the environment of a class should form its own characteristics, so that a hundred flowers can blossom in the campus. Class microclimate is directly related to the growth of students but also affects the school climate. Of course, the construction of campus culture cannot be separated from the creation of class characteristics in the construction of class culture. Then in reality, in order to facilitate management and evaluation, many schools require each class to be uniform, ignoring the creativity of students in each class. This practice deprives students of the right to think, choose and try, and even stifles the development of students' personality and creativity. Therefore, building a democratic and harmonious school environment is the key to encourage teachers and students to innovate.

(4) Pay attention to students' atmosphere and neglect teachers' team spirit

Students are the main body of campus culture and teachers are the dominant part of campus culture. In the activities of campus culture construction, teachers shoulder important responsibilities and missions. It is the teachers' duty to participate in the construction and activities of campus culture. Only by playing the leading role of teachers, can the quality of campus culture construction be improved. At present, some schools have the problem of attaching importance only to students' atmosphere and neglecting teachers' team spirit. In the construction of campus culture, we should not only emphasize the construction of good style of study but also pay attention to the construction of teachers' team spirit culture. Specifically, we can start with the construction of harmonious campus interpersonal relationships, including the relationship between cadres and the masses, teachers and teachers, teachers and students, students and students.

On the other hand, in view of the problems existing in the construction of campus culture, many researchers have put forward corresponding countermeasures, including the following.

The construction of campus culture should adhere to the Party's educational policy and help students establish a healthy outlook on life and values. The starting point and endpoint of campus culture are to improve the quality of teachers and students, train a generation of new people with ideals, morality, culture, and discipline, and better realize the Party's educational policy and training objectives.[13]

Make great efforts to cultivate a good school atmosphere and style of study. School atmosphere and style of study are potential educational forces with strong appeal, which can affect the whole school life and reflect the level of campus culture construction.[14] Attaching great importance to the construction of school network culture. Open up "ideological and political education website" on campus network, build network ideological position, and sing the main melody on the network.

Seek harmony in the conflict and rationally integrate contemporary campus culture. First of all, we should correctly handle the relationship between traditional culture and modern culture. The key to integrating the conflict between traditional culture and modern culture is to have a correct understanding and accurate evaluation of both. Second, we should correctly understand the peculiar blending of Eastern and Western cultures in the contemporary era. It is recognized that in the process of the development of human society and the process of extensive cultural exchanges, it is common and normal for different cultures to integrate and learn from each other. Third, aesthetic education should be strengthened to enrich the connotation of contemporary college culture.

Respect individual value and show humanistic care. As an indispensable part of university education and construction, the ultimate goal of campus culture is precisely the cultivation of creative talents, the enrichment of human nature education and the shaping of free and perfect personality. Human and human nature are the most basic concepts of the human world and the educational world. They constitute the logical starting point of an educational practice with humans as the main body and object.[15]

Establish a team of high-quality full-time and part-time campus culture construction. First, we should strive to build a full-time team of high-quality campus culture construction; second, we must build a part-time team of high-quality campus culture construction, which mainly includes two parts: the backbone of teachers and the backbone of students; third, we should build a high-quality team of students of campus culture construction.[16]

(6) The construction of campus culture should strengthen the sense of co-construction. The tasks of campus culture construction should be carried out among the staff of teachers and students, and their enthusiasm should be mobilized in order to accomplish them smoothly. Actively carry out colorful extracurricular activities.

---

[13]Bai Tongping. On University Culture [M]. Beijing: Beijing Forestry Press, 2000.

[14]Tu Junli, Zhang Zongye, Yang Changjiang. Preliminary Study on campus culture Construction [J]. Journal of Zhongzhou University, 2000 (S1):69–71.

[15]Chen Qiuyan. Rational Thoughts on College Culture Construction [J]. Educational Review, 2004 (4):43–45.

[16]Xue Wenzhi. Reflections on College Culture Construction [J]. China Higher Education Research, 2003 (5):21–23.

To carry out school cultural activities, we should not only strive for high-grade, multilevel, heavy participation and practical results, but also pay attention to the classification and guidance of ideological, scientific knowledge, cultural and entertainment activities.[17] The construction of campus culture should pay attention to "nurture people with culture". We should do a good job in the construction of campus culture and pay attention to cultivating and cultivating people through culture. The influence of culture is imperceptible and non-compulsory. Therefore, in cultural construction, we should overcome the idea of quick success and instant benefit and make unremitting efforts for a long time.[18]

Generally speaking, the concept of "cultural diversity" should be taken into account in the construction of campus culture, which brings challenges to school education. As an integral part of social and cultural construction, campus culture construction cannot ignore the cultural situation of the whole society in terms of purpose, content, and means. Otherwise, campus culture will lack the times and vitality, and cannot play its expected function. As the main object of school education is young students and citizens of the future society, it is particularly important to take necessary measures to educate them on cultural diversity for the protection and utilization of cultural diversity, the common intangible heritage of mankind. Therefore, the challenge of cultural diversity and the objective requirement of protecting cultural diversity should be taken into account in the construction of campus culture. Traditionally, the cultural function of schools is mainly embodied in the cultural inheritance, that is, to inherit the cultural wealth (history, language, stories, beliefs, knowledge, attitude toward life) of a country or its main ethnic group. It is not enough to inherit internal and external cultural diversity. If there is one, it is also through the transition and screening of the values that the state, the main ethnic group, and the dominant gender believe in. From the perspective of cultural diversity, this approach is not conducive to the definition of youth cultural diversity, to the cultivation of their awareness, appreciation, and respect for different cultures, and to the cultivation of awareness and ability of cross-cultural communication and understanding. Therefore, the construction of campus culture in the twenty-first century should rethink its own cultural stand and attitude, introduce the concept of cultural diversity, and contribute to the construction of a multi-coexistence cultural century.[19]

---

[17]Zhu Lixin. On the Shaping of Campus Spirit in Merged Colleges [J]. Jiangsu Higher Education, 2004 (1):99–101.

[18]Zhang Wenxian. Grasping the Core Elements and Refining the Spirit of Contemporary Chinese Universities [J]. China Higher Education, 2004 (1):13–14.

[19]Shi Zhongying. Responsibility and Pursuit of Educational Philosophy [M] Hefei: Anhui Education Press, 2007, 11:161.

6.4   Review of Chinese Studies on Campus Culture in Chinese Context

Present, there are many studies on campus culture in China. While reaching consensus, researchers have also explored campus culture from different aspects. These studies have laid a foundation and broadened our thinking for us to understand campus culture, discover its drawbacks, and rebuild campus culture. However, there are still some shortcomings in the study of campus culture, mainly as follows: there is no systematic theoretical system of campus culture construction, which makes the study of campus culture more confused and lack of direction; the existing research is rethinking, less empirical results; lack of timeliness; lack of in-depth research issues. In view of these problems, future research can proceed from the following aspects[20]:

First, pay attention to practice. Theory comes from practice and guides practice. On the one hand, the study of campus culture should proceed from reality and study the feasibility of the practical operation. On the other hand, although there are many new methods and ideas, they are not used in practice, mostly at the text level. Therefore, the study of campus culture should pay more attention to its practical significance, promote and try it out in schools, and play the original role of educational research.

Second, we should pay attention to the influence of extramural factors on campus culture. Campus culture is closely related to social culture. In building campus culture, we need to combine local spiritual style and make use of local high-quality resources. At the same time, good campus culture also has great radiating power on social culture, which complements each other. Therefore, in the study, we should not divide the scope into a small circle of schools but pay more attention to the social circle and study campus culture from the perspective of social culture. At the same time, we should not only pay attention to the status and role of teachers, principals, and students in the construction of campus culture, but also to the role of parents.

Finally, the school network culture is studied. This era is the era of the network. The network is affecting teachers and students' learning, work, and life extensively. School network culture emerges as the times require. Schools should establish a reasonable network culture, encourage teachers and students to actively use the network, collect resources and knowledge while avoiding the negative impact of the network.

---

[20]See footnote 4.

6.5   The Relationship Between Class Culture and Campus Culture

Relations between class and school

Class is an educational organization established by the school according to a certain number of students of the same age and educational level in order to achieve certain educational purposes. Class is the basic unit of a school and the most basic organization of school administration. Class teaching is the most representative form of modern education. A class is usually composed of one or more subject teachers and a group of students. The whole function of school education is mainly realized in class activities.

Relations between class culture and campus culture

Class culture is an important component of campus culture

Class culture is formed, accumulated, and condensed by class members (including students and teachers) in the course of class development and life. It is a set of ideals and beliefs, value orientation, ethics and morality, thinking mode, emotional attitude, aesthetic sentiment, behavior mode, and learning method that are generally accepted by class members. Class is the basic unit of school. Class culture belongs to campus culture. Class culture is an important part of campus culture. The construction of class culture is directly related to the growth of students but also affects the construction of campus culture.

The construction of campus culture is based on class culture

The construction of campus culture is based on class culture. In the sense of cultural ecology, class is a cultural and ecological organization composed of teachers and many students with different family culture backgrounds, community culture background, personality, and temperament. Classrooms are places where classes teach and students learn by themselves. Students spend 75% of their time in the classroom. The classroom constitutes a "cultural ecosphere". The advantages and disadvantages of the "cultural ecosphere" in this ecosphere directly affect the physical and mental health of teachers and students and the effect of education. Of course, the construction of campus culture can not be separated from the creation of class characteristics in the construction of class culture. Then in reality, in order to facilitate management and evaluation, many schools require each class to be uniform, ignoring the creativity of students in each class. This practice deprives students of the right to think, choose and try, and even stifles the development of students' personality and creativity. Faced with this situation, we should create a relaxed "big" environment of campus culture, stimulate the initiative of teachers and students, and enrich campus culture through the construction of diversified class culture.

Campus culture has a decisive influence on class culture

Campus culture has a decisive influence on class culture. It is not only the environment for the development and construction of class culture but also the source of the progress of class culture. Campus culture requires that the content of class culture can correspond to it. The constant advancement of campus culture construction will make the class culture change synchronously.

6.6   Case Studies on the Relationship Between Class Culture and Campus Culture

Case 1: Thoughts and perceptions caused by differences: a comparison between the two schools "I" teach[21]

In the past, class culture was very simple. There were only blackboard newspapers, contests, squadron names, and occasionally green plants to decorate the classroom for examination. There are almost no class theme activities, and the wall naturally does not need to arrange the relevant content. The whole school's ritual education is only "Entry, Tenth Birthday, Graduation Ceremony." Occasionally, a large-scale art festival is held by the school music teacher. As long as the head teacher cooperates with individual students to rehearse at the prescribed place, he does not need to participate in planning and rehearsal. After entering the new school, the campus culture is enriched and the quality requirements are much higher. For example, there is a large-scale art festival and sports meet every year, in which almost all the students participate, and all the teachers participate in the tasks of creating, directing, rehearsing and performing. There is a monthly festival, such as Science and Technology Festival, English Festival, Internet Surfing Festival, Sports Festival, and so on. In addition, there are some class-level activities such as "celebrating June 1st and New Year's Day" and grade-level activities such as "team entry, 10th birthday, graduation ceremony." "Reading Grade Examination" is conducted every month. Every month, we will evaluate the class of "Shuxiang" and "Lesser Pacesetters who are willing to learn and think well." The rich campus culture permeates into the class, and the class culture is also enriched. Besides the routine work of managing the class, there are also thematic activities determined according to the class characteristics, changes in the construction of class environment and culture, changes in class organization and operation mechanism......It constitutes a very large class life system, in which every student and teacher gets different degrees and aspects of development in school life and class life.

---

[21]Zhu Naimei et al. Interaction and Symbiosis: Research on the Mechanism of campus culture Transition [M]. Beijing: Educational Science Press, 2014 (3):126–127.

Case 2: Integration of campus culture and class culture[22]

After two years of school life, the students in our class are the third-grade students. In the first and second grades, we carried out class activities with the theme of small posts and small teams, respectively. The students' initiative and cohesion of the class have been improved, which laid the foundation for the activities to be carried out independently. After the third grade, under the leadership of the head of the grade group, we carefully studied and understood the characteristics of the students' years. We analyzed the commonness of the third-grade students and the personality of the students in the grade group. The third grade is a turning point in the five years of primary school. The students' independent consciousness is gradually increasing, but there is a lack of cooperation strategies and methods, which requires the conscious guidance of the teacher in charge of the class. We feel that the organizational structure of the second-grade class, which is based on teams, can no longer adapt to the characteristics of students' age development. Therefore, with the help of our collective efforts, we broke the single vertical organizational structure with teams as units, and set up six departments in the class, with the class committee as the center of the crisscross organizational structure of the class.

For example, for large-scale activities such as the Reading Festival, in the past, all classes carried out according to the theme of the school, activities are much the same, there is no difference between years, but also lack of class personality. Now the large-scale activities of the school are no longer directly decentralized to all classes, but after the discussion of the grade groups, according to the age characteristics of students, first determine the minor theme of the grade groups, and then plan by the six departments of the class independently. Every class has different students and departments. Of course, the planned activities have their own characteristics.

The school's Art Festival "Nurture the Childhood of Reading" opened again. How to combine the reading activities with the construction of the class department? How to carry out the special activities of the class, which are more popular with the students and more innovative in form? How to allow reading to keep up with the pace of the times so that students can read the essence of Chinese language and culture, read the truth of the people? Under the unified theme of the school, these problems should be in line with the age characteristics of students, combined with the actual class, play the role of six departments, so that students can become the masters of the activities. Under the collective efforts of the grade group, we agreed that the theme of the third grade of this reading Festival is "Reading Andersen's fairy tales and learning to be human." Because Andersen's fairy tales are very suitable for third-grade students in both text and content, third-grade students also need to learn some truth about life through such classical recitation. Therefore, all the teachers in our third-grade class agree to take this as a starting point to carry out the reading activities with class characteristics in departments, so that students can be baptized by both material and spiritual in the world of books. We set the general goal of the grade group for this activity as follows:

---

[22]Zhu Naimei et al. Interaction and Symbiosis: Research on the Mechanism of campus culture Transition [M]. Beijing: Educational Science Press, 2014 (3):156–159.

Through activities, let children like reading, let students understand Andersen, like his works.

Through activities, we can create a good reading atmosphere and improve our appreciation ability;

Through the activities, students can see, think about, and act out the profound truth brought by fairy tales, so as to put it into practice in their own actions;

Using the special organizational structure of the third-grade class—department, to improve students' comprehensive abilities of planning, organization, cooperation, communication, and so on;

This is a reading activity in which students in the class carry out special reading activities in various departments under the guidance of teachers.

(1) Knowledge activities organized by class committees:

Understanding Andersen's life and main works: The reason why Andersen's works are so shocking is that all his emotions are integrated into his works. His childhood was as insignificant as the ugly duckling he described in the ugly duckling and was looked down upon as well. In fact, ugly duckling is himself. In his works, he writes his dissatisfaction with the country and society. Of course, the third-grade students do not need to know a lot, but at least they know something about this great writer. So, we organize everyone to know his childhood, his great achievements and so on before reading his works. We use the 10-minute team meeting and a morning meeting to exchange our understanding of him. Recommended titles: The Emperor's New Dress, Wild Swan, Ugly Duckling, Daughter of the Sea, Thumbelina, Mother's Story, Butterfly, Snail, and Rose Book.

(2) Activities organized by the Ministry of Learning on seeing and thinking

Establishing the class book grading system, reading with problems, thinking. Students should borrow and answer questions in the school library and class book corner. In order to enable students to form a good habit of serious reading, each book in the library is accompanied by an answer card. After reading the book, students must complete the questions on the answer card before they can borrow the next book. After reading a book, a certain score will be obtained. Each reading score will be accumulated from two aspects: one is book score, which is based on the number of words borrowed by students (1 point per thousand words); the other is answer score, which is the score set by students of different years according to the difficulty of the book. The scores of books and answers are added up to the scores generated by borrowing books at a time.

(3) A performance organized jointly by the Ministry of Literature and Art and the Ministry of Sports

Through reading and reasoning alone, students still can not really appreciate the inspiration that books bring to people. Through questionnaires, we all feel that there is no new way to write experience, so this time the two departments of the Ministry of Arts and Sports boldly proposed whether these fairy tales can be transformed into textbooks plays and other forms of performance on the stage. Performing the stories in Andersen's Fairy Tales— the textbook play The Emperor's New Clothes and the dance play Wild Swan. Let the students learn how to be human in the performance.

Everyone was educated in the process of creating the program. It's more meaningful than just writing a few articles.

Step 1: the Ministry of Literature and Art writes textbook plays, and the teacher in charge of the class revises them;

Step 2: Sign up for the performance and choose the program according to your own special skills;

Step 3: Choose actors among the students who sign up;

Step 4: Rehearse the program with the support of the head teacher and music teacher;

Step 5: Show our achievements at the flag-raising ceremony.

(4) Finding activities organized by the Department of Regulations

Through reading Andersen's fairy tales, we can find out the story image in the class. If we can relate what we have learned to our real life, the significance of this activity will not only stay in reading but also set up and develop some excellent qualities and typical examples in the class. Therefore, according to the characters in fairy tales, the Department of Rules and Regulations first determines the models to be selected in the class: honest image ambassadors, kind ambassadors, brave little guards, diligent ambassadors, honest stars. Then through their own declaration, go to the stage to defend, students review the election, and finally select the representatives of these images. And on the wall, there are pictures and deeds of examples. We hope more students can learn from these examples.

(5) Ancillary activities

The Ministry of Environmental Protection organizes a series of activities: making bookmarks from waste materials and opening a bookmarking exhibition.

Activities organized by the Ministry of Health: Learning the library to make book cards for the books in the class book corner, standardize the borrowing system, carry out the activities of protecting books and whose books are the neatest.

Case 3: Students create campus culture[23]

Students can design their own class clothes, reflect their personality, but also organize more activities to give full play to students' uniforms, school uniforms, class uniforms, can also make their own class bookmarks, notebooks, class sculptures, and so on.

With students as the main body, let them combine their own age characteristics, design their favorite class layout, each class design its own characteristics, reflecting their own class culture.

Students can choose one of their favorite scientists, writers, and other historical celebrities. Name your class by their names and take him as an example for the whole class to learn and carry out a series of educational activities with his deeds as a carrier. Schools create different levels of display platform, so that students have

---

[23]Zhang Dongjiao. Evaluation by way of discussion: Beijing Experience in campus culture Construction [M]. Beijing: Beijing Normal University Press, 2016 (11):203–206.

the opportunity to exercise, class show, school show, go out to show, so that students become braver in the constant display.

Case 4: A case study of campus culture construction[24]

In the construction of campus culture, we have taken measures as follows:

(1) Give full play to students' autonomy. For example, the management of dormitories, the development of "honesty test" and so on. Due to a large number of high school students living in schools, the management of students living in schools is the responsibility of the student department. In the process of management, the formulation of dormitory regulations and the management of self-study in the evening fully respect the wishes of students and pay attention to their needs; and the development of "honesty test" makes the independent management of school students go to a new stage.

(2) Strengthen the construction of student unions and league committees. Due to historical reasons, the construction of student associations in schools is relatively poor. After the soft landing of the school, management attaches great importance to the management and construction of students' associations. Every year, the members of student unions and league committees are selected according to the procedure, and corresponding activities are formulated and strictly implemented. It should be said that the work of student unions and league committees at this stage is very standardized, and through a series of activities, such as lectures, learning, salons, ball games, speech, and debate competitions, which are close to the actual situation of students, students' centripetal force is condensed and their style is displayed.

(3) Enriching the spare–time life of teachers and students and carrying out various cultural and sports activities. As far as the school level is concerned, we carry out a large-scale literary and artistic performance every year to give full play to students' stylistic expertise. At the same time, we invite the community and superior leaders to attend and increase the social expansion of campus culture. As far as classes are concerned, classes use the time of Chinese and foreign festivals and team activities to design activities independently by students and carry out beneficial conversations, debates and other activities. In addition, the school also organizes and develops arts festivals, science and technology festivals, and other activities to display excellent works of art of teachers and students in the campus, making the campus full of strong artistic atmosphere. These measures make campus culture reflect the life pursuit and spiritual value of teachers and students, and also fully reflect the subjectivity and enthusiasm of teachers and students in the construction of campus culture.

---

[24]Xiang (2010).

References

Fan, R. (2014). Literature review on campus culture construction. *Journal of Northwest Adult Education College,* (3), 36–40.

Mao, L. (2008). Literature review on university campus culture. *Contemporary Education Forum (Macro Education Research),* (1), 31–32.

Shi, Z. (2007). *Responsibility and pursuit of educational philosophy* (Vol. 11, p. 161). Hefei: Anhui Education Press.

Xiang, H. (2010). *Theory and Practice of campus culture construction* (Vol. 7, p. 168). Hangzhou: Zhejiang University Press.

Xie, Y. (2006). *Research on the cultural construction of middle school.* Central China Normal University.

Chapter 7
Class Culture and Chinese Traditional Culture

This chapter concentrates on exploring the relations between class culture and Chinese traditional culture. Class culture is an important part of school culture. Class culture shows a class's unique spiritual outlook, which affects students' thinking, cognition and behavior, and dominates students' daily learning and life with a unique group reaction. Class culture represents the image of the class and reflects the life of the class. Class culture construction plays a key role in the development of the class.[1] The importance of class culture construction has been recognized more and more. Researchers began to actively explore new ideas of class culture construction. Some researchers have proposed to build a class culture based on traditional Chinese culture. Then, how about the research on traditional culture and class culture? Therefore, this study combines the relationship between class culture and traditional culture, and how to build a class culture based on traditional culture, in order to promote the further development of relevant research and practice.

The study of class culture in China began in the 1990s, but it did not attract enough attention from the academic circles at that time. Since 2001, with the implementation of a new round of curriculum reform, researchers have paid more and more attention to class culture. Up to now, the number of relevant studies has reached more than 1000 articles, mostly focusing on the content, function, and construction strategy of class culture. When discussing the strategies of class culture construction, the paper mainly focuses on the following three aspects:

First, the construction of class material culture. Class material culture is a carrier and physical support for the establishment and existence of a class. including the construction of class environment and class logo. Class environment is the spatial layout of the classroom, such as walls, blackboard newspapers, class motto posters, bulletin boards, learning gardens, classroom corners, and so on. The arrangement of the classroom environment should be aesthetic, make people feel happy, give people a sincere yearning, and sense of belonging, which is conducive to students'

---

[1] Zhang Ying. Read the "Three-character Classic" Well to Cultivate New People—A Useful Exploration of Developing the Cultural Construction of Characteristic Classes [J]. Huaxia Teachers, 2015 (10):14–15.

© Springer Nature Singapore Pte Ltd. 2020
X. Zhu and J. Li, *Classroom Culture in China*, Perspectives on Rethinking and Reforming Education, https://doi.org/10.1007/978-981-15-1827-0_7

devotion to learning and teachers' devotion to teaching. The class logo is one of the visual symbols of class culture, which generally includes two parts: class name, class motto, class song, class emblem, and other class spiritual symbols; and class uniform, class flag, and other material symbols. Each kind of sign construction has its unique significance and value, and also has different meanings and educational functions for students.

Second, the construction of the class system culture. The establishment and existence of classes need to be guaranteed by the system. Class system culture mainly includes two aspects: external system and internal system. The external system mainly refers to laws and regulations at the national level (such as the Education Law of the People's Republic of China), various policies and procedural rules issued by relevant state departments. The internal system mainly refers to the customs of local schools and the morals and rules of dealing with the world. They are more intangible systems, which are recognized by people and exist in people's mind. This unwritten rule has a great influence on students' behavior and thought.

Third, the construction of class spiritual culture. Class spiritual culture includes all areas of ideology, such as class atmosphere, class ethos, class spirit, class consensus, class common values, and so on. The core of class spiritual culture construction is the construction of class style, which is the embodiment of class spiritual outlook. To build a class style, first of all, we should strengthen the goal building, and let students feel the atmosphere of working for the same goal. Second, to create a good atmosphere of public opinion, students should have space and freedom to express their opinions, and teachers should guide students well. Third, the pursuit of educational equity is reflected in every stage of the class, in the beginning, in the middle, and in the end, every member can be treated fairly.[2,3]

At present, how to construct class culture has become a practical focus. Some researchers start with Chinese traditional culture and combine traditional culture with class culture construction.

7.1   Research Status of Chinese Traditional Culture

Since the Eighteenth National Congress of the Communist Party of China, the Party Central Committee, with Comrade Xi Jinping as its core, has attached great importance to cultural construction. It has placed the important position of inheriting excellent traditional culture, disseminating advanced socialist culture and building a strong cultural country in upholding and developing socialism with Chinese characteristics, thus demonstrating the distinct position and firm position of our Party in inheriting

---

[2]Tan Haiying. On the Role, Principles and Measures of Class Culture Construction [J]. Basic Education Research, 2013 (7):55–56.

[3]Ye Liu. On the Value, Strategies and Principles of Class Culture Construction [J]. Teaching and Management, 2019 (12):68–70.

excellent traditional culture. Since the reform and opening-up, the academic circles have made more and more comprehensive and in-depth research on traditional culture. Among them, the connotation, characteristics, value of the times, negative factors and creative transformation, and development of excellent traditional culture are the focus of researchers' attention.

Connotation of Chinese traditional culture

Chinese traditional culture is gradually inherited in the long history of development. It is a long-tested valuable resource with profound accumulation. Scholars have put forward different definitions of Chinese traditional culture. Zhang Dainian pointed out that Chinese traditional culture is mainly characterized by Confucian culture. The overall structure attaches great importance to ethical norms, while accommodating the cultures of other schools of thought and nationalities, which has the characteristics of pluralism. Chen Kaike pointed out that Chinese traditional culture is the cultural embodiment of the Chinese nation in the long historical process of change and development. The Confucian School of thought, represented by Confucius, is the dominant position. It also absorbs the essence of other cultures and forms an organic and harmonious cultural system.[4] In the book "Chinese Traditional Culture", Liu Fang, Zhong Jiande and Wang Yuhong define Chinese traditional culture as a culture formed and developed in the course of long-term historical development, retaining a stable form among the Chinese nation, including ideology, mode of thinking, value orientation, moral sentiment and etiquette system, customs and habits, ways of behavior, lifestyles, religious beliefs, literature and art, education, science and technology, cultural relics and classics, etc.[5] Liu Xiangxin, Liu Zhiyang, and Han Shutang define Chinese traditional culture as the main part of Chinese culture in the book "Marxism and Chinese Traditional Culture", which is also a rich historical heritage inherited by the ancestors. They record the history of the occurrence and evolution of the Chinese nation, as a way of thinking, values, codes of conduct, customs, and habits passed down from generation to generation, they permeate into the blood of every Chinese people. They are the sum of all kinds of the ideological culture of the Chinese nation, including all kinds of Ideological and material forms.[6] In the book "Chinese Traditional Culture", Zhang Qizhi defines traditional culture as not only ideological and cultural, but also historical relics, institutional culture, ancient books on literature, history, medicine, health, agriculture, astronomy, calendar, science and technology, as well as national customs, habits, and festivals, showing the characteristics of national culture.[7]

To sum up, the academic circles have different definitions of Chinese traditional culture, but the analysis of the content of Chinese traditional culture is basically the

---

[4]Lu Lijie. Construction of Class Culture in Secondary Vocational Schools Based on Traditional Culture Inheritance [D]. Zhejiang University of Technology, 2017.

[5]Liu Fang, Zhong Jiande, Wang Yuhong. Traditional Chinese Culture [M]. Beijing: China Media University Press, 2015:9.

[6]Liu Xiangxin, Liu Zhiyang, Han Shutang. Marxism and Chinese Traditional Culture [M]. Beijing: Social Science Literature Publishing House, 2009:4.

[7]See footnote 5.

same. They believe that traditional culture includes ideological culture, utensil culture, institutional culture, folk culture. and so on. It is the sum of material civilization and spiritual civilization created by the Chinese nation since its birth, which can be inherited to this day. It is the basis for the formation of the Chinese nation's way of thinking that emphasizes harmony, reorganization, intuition, relationship, and pragmatism, the value orientation that emphasizes righteousness but neglects profit, the conservative character and the way of dealing with etiquette and rules.

Characteristics of Chinese traditional culture

In the course of historical evolution, Chinese traditional culture presents remarkable characteristics different from other cultural forms. These characteristics are not only the unique spiritual attributes of Chinese traditional culture but also show the differences in cultural forms between the Chinese nation and other nationalities. Researchers have discussed the characteristics of Chinese traditional culture from the inside of traditional culture and the comparison with other cultural systems.

First, the theory of three characteristics. Taking Arab culture as a reference frame, Zhang Wenru reveals three characteristics of Chinese traditional culture by comparing with other cultural forms: premature maturity, the traditional culture formed a thinking paradigm of emphasizing life over nature more than two thousand years ago; independence, mainly manifested in the exclusion of foreign culture; introversion, focusing on the inner world, the development of traditional culture is mainly the continuous improvement of self-consciousness.[8]

Second, the theory of four characteristics. Gao Qi pointed out that Chinese traditional culture has the following four characteristics: first, it advocates practicality. The Chinese people have formed a pragmatic style of work in agricultural production for thousands of years, advocating hardship and hard work, practicing it physically, and opposing affectation, hyperbole, and formalism. In addition, Confucianism, which is dominant in traditional culture, actively advocates the concept of "joining life", advocates "officialdom is the natural outlet for good scholars", and attaches importance to the development of such practical disciplines as astronomy, mathematics, medicine, agriculture, and military science, which embodies the characteristics of pragmatism. Second, it emphasizes that the interests of groups are higher than those of individuals, which has the characteristics of integrity. The patriarchal clan system is the basic principle of dealing with the relationship between individual and individual, individual and group, group and group in ancient China. Under the influence of the patriarchal clan system, traditional culture embodies the characteristics that group value is higher than individual value, emphasizing the priority and importance of society and community to the individual. Third, we should attach importance to the harmonious relationship between man and nature, man and man, which has the characteristics of harmony and unity. Chinese traditional culture is rooted in agricultural civilization. It attaches great importance to the harmony and unity between man and nature, and then develops the harmony and unity between man and society as

---

[8]Zhang Wenru. Basic Characteristics of Humanistic Consciousness in Chinese Traditional Philosophy [J]. Academic Forum, 1999 (4):4–8.

well as the harmony of man's body and mind. Fourth, it pays attention to humanistic education and has the characteristics of advocating morality. Traditional culture has the characteristics of attaching great importance to ethics, and attaches great importance to moral cultivation centered on rites and music. Confucianism includes ways, methods, and contents of moral cultivation. "University" is the essence of Confucian classics. It systematically puts forward "Three Programmes" and "Eight Items", in which self-cultivation is the core content.[9]

Third, the theory of five characteristics. Wu Guang summed up the fundamental spirit of Chinese traditional culture as the moral and humanistic spirit of "people-oriented and virtue-oriented" and reshaped the core values of traditional culture as "One Way and Eight Virtues". On this basis, Wu Guang summarized the five characteristics of traditional culture: attaching importance to the moral subjectivity of moral rationality, people-oriented humanism, the integrity of diversity and harmony, the practicability, and the compatibility of open innovation are emphasized.[10]

Fourth, the theory of six characteristics. Liu Ruobin advocates that we need to explore regularly the development of traditional culture, and then recognize the six characteristics of traditional culture: Chinese traditional culture is the unity of unity and diversity, the unity of continuity and change, the unity of independence and accommodation. It follows the living mode of the unity of heaven and man, pursues the ideal moral personality of the best and the most beautiful, and follows the thinking mode of combining dialectical analysis with intuitive comprehension.[11]

The time value of Chinese traditional culture

Since the New Culture Movement, our country has experienced many scrutinies and reflections on the traditional culture. Once upon a time, the banner of cultural criticism of "overthrowing Confucian stores" and "criticizing Lin and Kong" was raised high, which spread the resentment of the frustration of modern China's backwardness and modernization to the traditional culture created by the sages, and the irrational criticism and even the total denial of traditional culture once became a quite market-oriented social trend of thought. Until the Communist Party of China made the political choice of inheriting excellent traditional culture to condense the national spirit, we began to treat Chinese traditional culture dialectically with a rational attitude, not only acknowledging the historical role of traditional culture, but also thinking about the dross contained in it, paying more attention should be paid to exploring the ideological value and practical significance of excellent traditional culture in modern society through innovation and transformation.

The study of the value of traditional culture in the era is mainly carried out from two perspectives. On the one hand, interpreting the contemporary value of traditional culture from a macro perspective, identifying with the cognitive path of the unity

---

[9]Gao Qi. Research on the Value of Traditional Culture in Civil Moral Education [D]. Jilin University, 2018.

[10]Wu Guang. The Core Idea of Chinese Traditional Culture and Its Contemporary Value [J]. Social Science Front, 2013 (2):1–6.

[11]Liu Ruobin. On the Main Contents and Characteristics of Chinese Traditional Culture [J]. Dong Yue Lun Cong, 2008 (2):194–197.

of knowledge and practice nurtured by excellent traditional culture, the ideal pursuit of the great harmony world, the people-oriented political intention and the new political wisdom of reforming the past, not only embodies the inevitable trend of China's historical development, but also has become the value guide of modernization. Chen Zhanguo discussed the effect of Chinese traditional culture on the whole. He believed that the rich and harmonious thoughts contained in Chinese traditional culture, such as keeping harmony, putting people first, respecting morality and righteousness, and tolerating everything with the highest virtue, had a promoting effect on social stability, democratic politics, economic development, and spiritual civilization construction.[12] Under the new situation of increasingly fierce international competition and coexistence of opportunities and challenges for national development, we should attach importance to the function of traditional culture in "cultural adjustment in the great turning point of history."[13] We should further explore the excellent cultural heritage of the Chinese nation, inherit and carry forward the excellent moral tradition, so as to enhance national cohesion and competitiveness.

On the other hand, the positive role of Chinese traditional culture in today's social fields is analyzed from the micro perspective. First, traditional culture provides ideological resources for the socialist democratic political road. Wang Yanqiao holds that "devoting knowledge to practice and applying knowledge to practice" provides the ideological basis for "integrating theory with practice", and "tolerating everything with the highest virtue" achieves the openness of the democratic political road. The Confucian humanism concept lays the foundation for the political proposition and political system of "putting people first" and "governing the country by virtue" put forward and practiced by our Party.[14] Tian Keqin reveals the practical significance of excellent traditional culture to the socialist democratic political road. He holds that socialist reform inherits and develops the traditional Chinese reform thought, that socialist national unification thought carries forward and develops the fine tradition of patriotism, and that under the background of comprehensively promoting the rule of law, the thought of governing the country by combining etiquette with law has important enlightenment for the present, and can provide useful reference for the construction of a civilized China ruled by law.[15]

Second, traditional culture provides value nourishment for the construction of socialist advanced culture. Zheng Wentang believes that there are essential differences between traditional culture and socialist culture, but there are similarities between them, such as "the unity of the world" and the principle of material unity, "the

---

[12]Chen Zhanguo. Excellent Chinese Traditional Culture and Harmonious Society [J]. Beijing Social Science, 2005 (3):3–8.

[13]Ji Guiqi. Cultural Adjustment in the Great Turn of History: On Dong Zhongshu's Integration and Development of Confucian Culture [J]. Journal of Shandong Normal University (Humanities and Social Sciences Edition), 2015, 60 (3):33–67.

[14]Wang Yanqiao. Traditional Culture and Theoretical Construction of Socialism with Chinese Characteristics [J]. Journal of Party School of Zhejiang Provincial Party Committee of the Communist Party of China, 2013, 29 (1):108–112.

[15]Tian Keqin. Socialism with Chinese Characteristics and Chinese Traditional Culture [J]. Hubei Social Science, 2014 (1):5–9.

theory of yin and yang" and the law of unity of opposites, "the unity of reason and situation" and the historical materialism, "the practical application of the world" and the practical viewpoint. These similarities enable the excellent traditional culture to inject nutrients into the construction of advanced culture.[16] Chen Weiping expounded the ways and paths of integrating excellent traditional culture into advanced socialist culture, emphasized that advanced culture should critically inherit traditional culture, combine traditional culture's ideas of moderation and change with reform and opening-up, endow it with new connotation and vitality, and realize the fundamental transformation of cultural paradigm from the old to the new, and promote the great development and prosperity of socialist culture.[17]

Third, the traditional culture provides the idea to follow for the construction of a socialist ecological civilization. Li Zuyang believes that the traditional culture contains rich ecological wisdom, such as harmonious coexistence of nature and man, respect for the inherent law of nature, and humanism of reverence for life. The traditional culture nurturing modern ecological ethics provides the ideological source for the choice and practice of socialist ecological civilization with Chinese characteristics.[18] An Qinian[19] and Tang Meijiang,[20] respectively, elaborated the ways of settling body and mind in traditional culture, the spiritual purpose of Confucian ecological ethics of harmony between man and nature, the unity of people and things, the timeliness and the moderate ecological ethics, the ecological cultural paradigm of Taoism's "non-sentient-beings have the Buddha-nature" and "Taoism follows nature", which are of great significance and value for solving ecological crisis and strengthening the construction of ecological civilization.

Fourth, traditional culture provides spiritual resources for cultivating and practicing socialist core values. Xiao Guiqing believes that the cultivation and promotion of core values must be based on excellent traditional culture, absorb the nutrition of excellent traditional culture, and make it an important source of maintaining core values.[21] Fang Xiaozhen pointed out that we should adhere to the unity of tradition and modernity, nationality and cosmopolitan, dominance and diversity, keep pace with the times and inherit tradition, realize the inheritance and transcendence of

---

[16]Zheng Wentang, Hua Yuwu, Gao Jianwei. On the Internal Connection between the Theory of Socialism with Chinese Characteristics and the Excellent Traditional Chinese Culture [J]. Research on Ideological Education, 2012 (9):36–39.

[17]Chen Weiping. Constructing Socialist Culture with Chinese Characteristics and Critically Inheriting Traditional Culture [J]. Journal of Shanghai Jiaotong University (Social Science Edition), 2001 (1):3–7.

[18]Li Zuyang, Wei Junguo. On Environmental Ethics in Chinese Traditional Culture [J]. Academic Exploration, 2003 (1):93–96.

[19]Shao Peng, An Qinian. Eco-ethics in Chinese Traditional Culture and Its Contemporary Enlightenment [J]. Theoretic Monthly, 2014 (4):69–72.

[20]Tang Meijiang. The Way of Traditional Physical and Psychological Settlement and the Construction of Contemporary Ecological Civilization: Reflections on the Modern Value of Chinese Excellent Traditional Culture [J]. Modern Philosophy, 2013 (5):118–124.

[21]Han Zhongmin. On the Internal Connection between Chinese Excellent Traditional Culture and Socialist Core Values [J]. Journal of Guangdong Vocational and Technical College of Water Conservancy and Electricity, 2016, 14 (1):77–80.

core values to excellent traditional culture, and carry forward excellent traditional culture in the process of scientific construction of core value system.[22] Qi Weiping emphasized that the cultivation and practice of core values must attach importance to the dual concern of traditional culture nourishment and modernity growth, activate the nourishing value of traditional culture by modernity growth, and realize the integration and innovation of traditional culture through modernity development.[23]

Negative factors in Chinese traditional culture

Chinese traditional culture, based on agricultural production, relies on natural conditions and human relations to form perceptual knowledge with nature as its direct object and political norms based on family ethics. The ethical nature of traditional culture determines its basic value pursuit of "inner saints and outer kings". On the basis of industrialization, modernization has got rid of excessive dependence on nature and created a modern civilization different from the traditional one. Modern civilization is characterized by knowledge and technology, is based on commodity economy, and aims at freedom, equality, rule of law, and democracy. It can be seen that there must be some gap between traditional culture and modernization. Some scholars believe that traditional culture is the resistance or barrier to the development of modernization.[24]

Li Shenzhi distinguishes "traditional culture" from "cultural tradition" and holds that "traditional culture" is the sum of all kinds of cultural phenomena in China since ancient times, including all the cultural phenomena that have not disappeared. "Cultural tradition" is unchangeable, its influence runs through almost all traditional cultures, and dominates the behavior, thought, and soul of the Chinese people. In his view, the main reason for China's stagnation is that our autocratic cultural tradition is too deep and the vitality of autocracy is too tenacious.[25] Guo Qiyong pointed out that the theory of "Confucian Renaissance" underestimated the great negative impact of Confucian culture on history and reality. For example, Confucianism's tradition of annotating classics and introverted psychology easily lead to dogmatism. Confucianism pays more attention to practice than theory, less logic and more insight, which also easily leads to the proliferation of empiricism. Since the Qin and Han Dynasties, the structure and function of Confucianism have fundamentally been conducive to the maintenance of feudal monarchy and cultural autocracy. The combination of this

---

[22]Fang Xiaozhen. Analysis of the Relation between Socialist Core Values and Chinese Excellent Traditional Culture [J]. Introduction to Ideological and Theoretical Education, 2015 (11):65–67.

[23]Qi Weiping, Xu Wei. Traditional Culture Nurturing and Modernity Growth of Socialist Core Values [J]. Research on Clean Government Culture, 2015, 6 (4):91.

[24]Wang Zengfu. Research Progress and Prospect of Chinese Traditional Culture [J]. Learning and Practice, 2017 (10):112–121.

[25]Li Shenzhi. Chinese Cultural Tradition and Modernization [J]. Strategy and Management, 2000 (4):1–12.

tradition with the small-scale peasant consciousness, patriarchal ideology, bureaucratic style, and red tape, which still has vitality, will inevitably constitute a great resistance to modernization.[26]

In the view of some foreign scholars, traditional culture has shown more negative values in the process of social development in China. Max Weber believes that Chinese traditional culture lacks a spirit similar to Western Protestant ethics. It does not allow people to transform the world, but advocates people to adapt to the order and customs of the world. Therefore, Confucian ethics is the main obstacle to the rapid development of China's modernization. Du Weiming emphasized that Chinese traditional culture, especially the Confucian tradition and the value orientation it represents, not only did they not bring the peak of science and technology and democracy to China, but also played an obstacle role in fact.[27]

American modernization expert Blake pointed out that modernization is the evolution of traditional society to modern society. It is the most difficult to realize modernization in an old and mature traditional society like China, because the traditional culture is a heavy burden for China to realize modernization.[28] Other scholars questioned the motivation and effect of the Chinese government in promoting the inheritance and innovation of traditional culture, especially the promotion of Chinese culture going out through Confucius Institutes.

Evaluation principles of Chinese traditional culture
In dealing with Chinese traditional culture, we should make the past serve the present and bring forth the new, inherit and develop the essence of traditional culture, making Chinese traditional culture serve the practice of administering the country, act on the shaping of new socialist people and promote the building of a harmonious socialist society. This is related to what criteria we should adopt to distinguish the essence and dregs of traditional culture. Only by defining the objective criteria of discrimination can we know which of the traditional cultures are to be inherited and promoted and which are to be criticized and eliminated. Only in this way can we oppose both cultural retro-classicism and cultural nihilism in the process of studying traditional cultures. At present, scholars mainly put forward five basic principles for evaluating traditional culture.

First, the practical principle of "science-progress" is represented by Zhang Dainian.[29] This view is based on the reality of social production and life. It holds that the excellent traditional culture is the one that has a wide influence on the current social practice, encourages the progress of the people, promotes social development and is accepted by the majority of the people. This principle embodies the sense of responsibility for social development, and shows strong practical rationality.

---

[26]Guo Qiyong. Modernization and Chinese Traditional Culture [J]. Journal of Wuhan University (Social Science Edition), 1986 (5):9–14.

[27]Du Weiming. Yi Yang Lai Fu [M]. Shanghai Literature and Art Publishing House, 1997.

[28]C.E. Blake. Motivation of Modernization: A Study of Comparative History [M]. Zhejiang People's Publishing House, 1989.

[29]Zhang Dainian. Basic Spirit of Chinese Culture [J]. Qilu Academic Journal, 2003:5.

Second, the principle of "Marxist guidance" is represented by Chen Xianda.[30] This standard requires us to criticize, inherit, and carry forward Chinese traditional culture under the guidance of Marxism, because only under the guidance of Marxist scientific world outlook and methodology and following the basic standpoint of dialectical materialism and historical materialism, can we activate the high-quality resources in traditional culture and adhere to the socialist direction in cultural construction.

Third, the principle of "structural analysis" is represented by Zhang Liwen.[31] This standpoint starts with cultural structure and deeply analyses the surface structure, deep structure, and overall structure of Chinese traditional culture from both macro and micro perspectives. It also analyses all levels of cultural structure, combs various elements of diverse and inclusive structure, open and complementary structure and practical structure, and advocates the sublation of traditional culture in every system, structure, and level.

Fourth, the principle of "rational baptism" is represented by Chen Weiping.[32] This standard requires that we should focus on philosophy theory, adhere to the principle of rationality supremacy and base ourselves on others' point of view, use instrumental rationality and value rationality, scientific knowledge system, rigorous logic, and modern humanistic value scale, consider the occurrence mechanism, characteristics and deep connotation of traditional culture, and then we can evaluate the value of traditional culture in an all-round way.

Fifth, the principle of "excellent cultural characteristics" is represented by Li Zonggui.[33] He pointed out that those that conform to excellent cultural characteristics belong to excellent traditional culture, which are mainly manifested in four aspects: reflecting the positive aspects of the national spirit, reflecting the spiritual direction of Chinese cultural health; having the great role of stimulating national self-confidence and pride; assuming the function of national cultural identity; and having historical inheritance and stability, it still has strong vitality today.

Sixth, the principle of "cultural value" is represented by Chen Lai.[34] This view holds that the evaluation of traditional culture must go beyond the utilitarian stand-point, focusing not only on the present but also on the long-term development and all-round development of culture, judging the advantages and disadvantages of tra-ditional culture from the standpoint of cultural value, judging the value of traditional culture from the standpoint of inherent development of culture itself, and judging the significance of traditional culture from the standpoint of human nature and the

---

[30]Chen Xianda. Contemporary Value of Chinese Traditional Culture [J]. Chinese Social Sciences, 1997:2.

[31]Zhang Liwen, Tingtian Sanlang. Traditional Culture and East Asian Society [J]. Renmin University Press, 1992:13–22.

[32]Chen Weiping. Introduction: Talking about Tradition and Value [M]. Shanghai Literature and Art Publishing House, 1991.

[33]Li Zonggui. Excellent Cultural Tradition and National Cohesion [J]. Philosophical Research, 1992:3.

[34]Chen Lai. Tradition and Modernity: A Humanist Perspective [M]. Life, Reading and New Knowledge Triple Bookstore, 2009.

needs of life and systematic development of social culture and the intrinsic value of culture itself.

Creative transformation and development of excellent traditional culture
There are both essence and dross in Chinese traditional culture. The essence of traditional culture, that is, the fine traditional culture, should be inherited and developed. The holistic study of creative transformation and innovative development of traditional culture (referred to as "double creation") in academic circles began when General Secretary Xi Jinping visited Shandong and listened to the speeches of Qufu and Confucius Research Institute. After that, the discussion of "double creation" of traditional culture gradually became a hot topic. Combining with the modern analysis of the Confucian idea of "cultivating oneself, regulating the family and ruling the world", academia attaches great importance to the "exploration and utilization of traditional cultural resources" and "creative transformation".[35] At present, the research on "double creation" of excellent traditional culture mainly concentrates on three fields.

One is the definition of "double creation". Yang Yiqin[36] and Wang Yilin[37] believe that creative transformation is to transform those connotations and outmoded forms of expression that still have reference value, endow them with new connotations and modern forms of expression, and activate their vitality in accordance with the characteristics and requirements of the times; Innovative development is to make new developments in accordance with the new progress of the times, to supplement, expand, and improve the connotation of Chinese excellent traditional culture, and to enhance its influence and appeal. If it is said, in diachronicity, creative transformation is how to move from the past to the present, then innovative development is how to move from the present to the future, how to endow the tradition with modern life, and promote its development and perfection.

Second, the basic principles and requirements of "double creation". Shang Zhixiao pointed out that the "double creation" of excellent traditional culture should follow four basic principles: fully respecting traditional culture, consciously respecting the history of the nation, differentiating the essence and dross scientifically, differentiating the advantages and disadvantages, playing a role in reality, serving the current social development, transforming and redeveloping to rich development, and endowing new connotation of the times.[38] Yu Yuanpei believes that the creative transformation of traditional culture needs to be based on reform practice and combine "national conditions" with "world conditions". We should look at the problem as a

---

[35]Shi Xiaohong, Miao Yongquan. Modern Analysis of the Confucian Idea of "Cultivating Oneself, Regulating the Family and Ruling the World" and Exploration and Utilization of Traditional Cultural Resources [J]. Journal of Shandong Normal University, 2015:2.

[36]Yang Yiqin. Socialist Core Values: Double Creative Development of Excellent Traditional Culture [J]. Chinese Journal of Social Sciences, 2014:9.

[37]Wang Yilin. Xi Jinping's Creative Transformation and Innovative Development of Chinese Traditional Culture [J], Party Literature, 2016:1.

[38]Shang Zhixiao. Philosophical Reflection on Creative Transformation and Innovative Development [J]. Guangming Daily, 2017:1.

whole and avoid "fragmentation". We should dialectically distinguish it and stick to critical inheritance. We should carry forward the national spirit with patriotism as the core and prevent cultural closure.[39]

Third, the basic way and path of "double creation". From Zhang Xiaowen 's point of view, we should adhere to the guidance of Marxism and create a systematic, stable and special discourse system on the basis of paying attention to combing traditional culture, so as to integrate national elements with world languages, and finally integrate into experience life, so as to truly realize "double creation".[40] Sun Xiguo regards "double creation" as a diachronic systematic project, and believes that it can only be completed through four links: historical interpretation, critical inheritance, comprehensive innovation, and practical transcendence.[41] Xi Ge emphasized that the key to realizing the "double creation" of excellent traditional culture lies in the integration of inheritance and innovation, the preservation of cultural innovation by cultural inheritance, and the deepening of cultural inheritance by cultural innovation. He also focused on the following four aspects: setting up the standards for the transformation of traditional culture, combining traditional culture with real life, and activating the modern connotation of traditional culture and developing traditional culture facing the world.[42]

Over the past 30 years, many valuable ideas and fruitful achievements have been formed in the study of Chinese traditional culture and its modernization. However, the study on promoting and innovating Chinese excellent traditional culture still needs to be strengthened. Specifically, why should Chinese traditional culture inherit and develop, whether it can inherit and inherit, what are the criteria for inheritance and development, and why innovation and transformation after inheritance are possible are all issues to be discussed.

7.2 The Relation Between Class Culture and Chinese Traditional Culture

Culture is a system of values and meanings shared by a group or society, including material entities that make these values and meanings concrete. Both Chinese traditional culture and class culture belong to the category of culture. They influence each other. On the one hand, traditional culture promotes the construction of class culture,

---

[39] Yu Yuanpei. Reflections on the Creative Transformation of Traditional Culture [J]. Journal of Ningbo Municipal Party School, CCP, 2014:3.

[40] Zhang Xiaowen. Promoting the Creative Transformation of Traditional Culture in the Process of Modernization [J]. Xuehai, 2015:5.

[41] Yan Zhenyu, Sun Xiguo. Reflections on the Path of Creative Transformation of Traditional Culture [J]. Socialism with Chinese Characteristics. 2015:6.

[42] Xi Ge, Zhang Wu. To Carry Forward the Core Values and Realize the Creative Transformation of Traditional Culture [J]. Guangming Daily, 2015:2.

on the other hand, class culture influences the inheritance and development of traditional culture. Researchers have explored the relationship between class culture and traditional culture from these two aspects.

The promotion of traditional culture to class culture
Chinese traditional culture is an important resource for the construction of class culture. It is conducive to comprehensively improving students' comprehensive quality, cultivating excellent quality. Class culture which absorbs Chinese traditional culture has strong vitality and influence, and plays an important role in improving students' comprehensive quality.[43] Focusing on the role of traditional Chinese culture in promoting class culture, the researchers mainly carry out research in three ways: starting from the macro level, discussing the role of traditional culture in the construction of class culture; starting from the micro level, focusing on the role of specific content of traditional culture in the construction of class culture; focusing on the role of traditional culture of different schools in the construction of class culture.

On the macro level, the role of traditional culture in promoting class culture can be summarized as that traditional culture is the "soul" and "source" of class culture. Chinese traditional culture is formed and gathered in the process of continuous development and transformation of Chinese civilization, which reflects the national characteristics, culture, and customs. In the history of national development, concepts, forms, and ideological culture are the most important manifestations. Chinese traditional culture is created by the ancestors in life and production and inherited by the Chinese nation. It has a long history, broad and profound, and all-inclusive characteristics. Introducing traditional culture into the construction of class culture can make the content of class culture more fully and inherit excellent traditional culture. The introduction of traditional culture in the process of class culture construction makes the culture collide and promote each other, promotes the construction of class culture closer to the local cultural tradition, and enhances the interest and local characteristics of class culture. It can also enable students to better understand Chinese traditional culture, consciously inherit Chinese traditional culture, find common ground with national culture, and constantly enhance national self-confidence.[44] Lan Haiyan pointed out that the integration of traditional culture into the construction of class culture is conducive to creating a cultural class, making the class more cohesive.[45] Yu Pan pointed out that taking class culture as the carrier and taking excellent traditional culture as the content can promote the development of students in class, form the characteristic class culture under the vision of excellent traditional culture, and promote the formation of students' good character.[46] Jin Qing pointed out that building class culture with traditional culture is an invisible educational

---

[43] See footnote 4.

[44] See footnote 4.

[45] Lan Haiyan. Exploration of the Integration of Traditional Culture and Class Culture Construction [J]. Primary School Teaching Reference, 2018 (33):85–86.

[46] Yu Pan. Infiltrating the Students' life Background with Excellent Traditional Culture: A study on the Construction of Class Culture in Colleges and Universities from the Perspective of Excellent Traditional Culture [J]. Journal of Changji University, 2019 (02):78–81.

model for shaping students' correct outlook on life and values.[47] Traditional culture is the source of building class culture, especially the local culture with local characteristics. It is a very good way to construct class culture with the help of local traditional culture. Introducing Chinese traditional culture into the construction of class culture is the reuse of precious resources.[48]

On the micro level, various specific traditional cultures also play a role in promoting class culture. Tang Fanhong pointed out that excellent traditional culture can nourish and construct class culture to promote students' healthy growth and improve their comprehensive quality. Specifically speaking, the classics of Chinese classics are the crystallization of the wisdom of ancient sages, and attaching importance to wisdom and morality, and emphasizing the cultivation of cultural and humanistic qualities are the core of class culture. Reading classics is conducive to cultivating students' sentiments and enriching class culture. In the construction of class culture, through the integration of traditional filial piety education, let students feel filial piety, sense filial piety, practice filial piety, can achieve the effect of improving class cultural quality.[49] Li Kaiyi pointed out that class culture is the spiritual power to guide and edify students, and "harmony" is a very important concept in Chinese philosophy. It is the criterion of friendly coexistence between people and the premise of cooperation. Introducing "harmony" culture into the construction of class culture can strengthen students' sense of belonging to the class and constructing harmonious class collective.[50] Peng Yanghua pointed out that traditional culture plays an extremely important role in shaping the common heart of the nation. It is a bridge to communicate the soul of the people of the nation. Learning and inheriting excellent traditional culture can enhance people's sense of belonging, build up people's national self-esteem, self-confidence, and build a sense of historical responsibility of socialism with Chinese characteristics. Traditional culture should become a necessary part of patriotic education and an indispensable part of class culture construction.[51] Yu Pan pointed out that Chinese traditional culture includes the spirit of emphasizing morality, pragmatism, self-improvement, tolerance, and patriotism. Combining these with class culture and education, students can enhance their humanistic literacy and spiritual pursuit through explicit and implicit class culture atmosphere.[52] Yu Pan pointed out that in the Analects of Confucius, "the use of propriety, harmony is precious" guides students to take harmony as precious; "Mencius Liang Hui Wang" advocates the feeling of fraternity between the old and

[47] Jin Qing. Research on the Path of Chinese Traditional Culture in the Construction of Class Culture [J]. Drama House, 2017 (23):127–128.

[48] See footnote 4.

[49] Tang Fanhong. Practical Exploration of Traditional Culture in Class Culture Construction [J]. Curriculum Education Research, 2017 (16):216.

[50] Li Kaiyi. A New Form of Class Development Based on "Harmony: Culture: Strategies for Promoting Class Cohesion [J]. Moral Education in Primary and Secondary Schools, 2018 (12):65–66.

[51] Peng Yanghua, Lai Changming. Excellent Traditional Culture and Construction of Class Culture in Universities [J]. Journal of Southern Metallurgical College, 1999 (5):59–61+65.

[52] See footnote 46.

the old, the young and the young; Confucius proposed that "brothers are all within the four seas". These traditional cultures contain the beliefs of friendship, fairness, and honesty. It can improve students' self-cultivation and create a harmonious and enterprising class atmosphere and a fair and friendly learning atmosphere.[53] Zhao Lu pointed out that Chinese culture is extensive and profound, and each region has its own unique cultural resources, such as Han culture, Guanlong culture, Bashu culture, Central Plains culture, Songliao culture, Wuyue culture, Jingchu culture, and Lingnan culture. According to the characteristics of the local culture, we can make good use of the historical relics of the local culture to carry out the corresponding class culture construction.[54] Lu Lijie pointed out that local folk culture, as a traditional culture with local characteristics, has strong regionalism and special rituals, which can enhance the interest of class culture, enrich the content of class culture, and improve the quality of class culture.[55] Zou Ke pointed out that in the construction of class culture, taking traditional festivals as the carrier and absorbing the cultural elements of traditional festivals, students can feel the charm and power of culture in the process of imperceptible influence, which is indelible for students.[56]

Chinese traditional culture is a complex. Confucianism attaches great importance to ethics, Taoism emphasizes speculation, Mohism pushes logic, Legalism favors the rule of law, soldiers talk about war, farmers are good at farming, and Confucianism, law, and Taoism are the main ideological factions. Some researchers focus on the role of the traditional culture of different schools in the construction of class culture, and discuss the role of Confucianism, Taoism, and Legalism in the construction of class culture.

Confucianism has deeply influenced the development and process of Chinese history, is the basis of building a harmonious society, and has a strong role in promoting the construction of harmonious class culture.[57] Chen Cunjing bases his research on the relationship between Confucianism and harmonious culture, and believes that Confucianism can effectively promote the construction of harmonious class culture.[58] Jiang Guangrong,[59] Ge Zhaoguang,[60] Feng Ge[61] and others have put forward

---

[53] See footnote 52.

[54] Zhao Lu. How to Integrate the Excellent Traditional Culture into the Cultural Construction of Colleges and Universities [J]. Journal of Tianjin Sino-German Vocational and Technical College, 2015 (6):79–80.

[55] See footnote 4.

[56] Zou Ke. Promoting Traditional Culture and Constructing Class Culture—Preliminary Study on the Integration of Traditional Festivals and Class Culture [J]. Educational Observation (Second Half Month), 2017, 6 (5):61+91.

[57] Xue Mingyang, Introduction to Chinese Traditional Culture. Volume 1 [M]. Fudan University Press, 2003.

[58] Chen Cunjing, Reflections on Class Culture Construction [J]. Jilin Education, 2013 (2):117.

[59] Jiang Guangrong, Research on Class Social Ecological Environment [M]. Central China Normal University Press, 2002.

[60] Ge Zhaoguang. Lectures on Ancient Chinese Culture [J]. Book Store, 2006 (10):60.

[61] Feng Ge. Study on the Strategy of Modern Harmonious Class Construction Based on Confucian Harmonious Culture [D]. Nanjing Normal University, 2011.

similar ideas in their research. They believe that Confucian culture, which emphasizes morality, harmony, and righteousness, can unconsciously improve students' accomplishment and moral quality, and get along with their classmates in friendship and mutual assistance, so that they can take into account the overall situation and work hard to safeguard collective honor, thus promoting harmony in the class. Based on the idea of "people-oriented", Yeliu pointed out that the class is a free world for students and the students are the masters of the class. Class culture plays a direct role in educating students. The construction of class culture should be student-oriented, respect the law of students' life growth, attach importance to the exertion and development of personality potential, meet students' legitimate and reasonable psychological development needs, actively encourage students to exert their inherent potential, and create their own class cultural content. When designing the content of class culture construction, we should always put students in the main position, give full play to students' subjectivity, and let students become designers, participants, and implementers of class culture construction.[62] Yu Ronghua pointed out that the construction of class culture needs the spiritual connotation of self-improvement. In Zhouyi Dazhuan, there are two famous sayings: "Heaven walks strong, gentlemen strive constantly for self-improvement," "the terrain is vast, gentlemen carry things with great virtue." With the rapid development of China's economy and the increasing improvement of people's material life, primary school students growing up in the greenhouse should cultivate the national spirit of self-improvement, which has become the top priority of class teachers' work. The class teachers must teach by their own words and deeds. This is also a basic vane for every member of a class to be able to grow up in the future.[63] Liu Lina pointed out that "benevolent people love others" is one of the core contents of Confucianism. The answer of contemporary teaching work is to pay attention to humanizing in education. In the construction of class culture, the humanistic sentiment is an indispensable important factor. Because there are some differences in students' actual situation and family background, we should actively integrate humanistic content into the current cultural construction work. Students' appearance and daily behavior are the most important contents in the construction of class culture. Teachers should actively practice Confucianism's "etiquette", so that students have good manners, and implement "etiquette" into students' daily life. Based on the belief of Neo-Confucianism,[64] Deng Shuang believes that the ideal humanistic society must be belief. The foundation of class culture construction is to establish a correct outlook on life and values, and form a positive belief in order to enhance the individual spirit.[65]

---

[62] See footnote 3.

[63] Yu Ronghua. Application of Confucianism in the Construction of Class Culture in Primary Schools [J]. New Curriculum Research. 2011 (04):77–78.

[64] Liu Lina. The Embodiment of Confucianism in the Construction of Class Culture [J]. Curriculum Education Research, 2018 (41):189.

[65] Deng Shuang, Zhao Baisen. The Role of the Humanistic Spirit of Neo-Confucianism in the Construction of Class Culture [J]. Education and Teaching Forum, 2013 (6):230–231.

The core of Taoist thought is "governing by doing nothing". On the premise of highly respecting and following the natural law, we will not impose too much subjective will on the development of things, but let them develop independently.[66] Mou Zongsan and Feng Tianyu pointed out that Taoist culture is the crystallization of our unique wisdom and the immortal source of Chinese traditional culture. In the "natural" beautiful environment to better promote human growth. No one can exist without the environment. Every student needs to grow up in a certain environment. The Taoist concept can make us clearly realize the importance of classroom environment, and then create a harmonious environment to edify students, make them develop physically and mentally in an all-round way, while maintaining the neatness of the environment.[67]

Legalists in traditional culture attach great importance to the system, whose core idea is "rule of law". For a class, rules and regulations are very important. Only by relying on strict and standardized rules and regulations to manage, can it become a unified and orderly class.[68] Both Lin Jincai and Guo Yi mentioned the use of "rule of law" to build a strict class system culture. The construction of class culture must absorb the concept of law in traditional culture, formulate some scientific system norms, and restrain students' behavior through these system norms.[69,70] Zhong Huijuan,[71] Gong Xiaoyun,[72] Lu Xiaoxia[73], and others have made in-depth research on the role of Legalist culture in the construction of class culture. They believe that only by defining the system norms can students' behavior be followed by "rules". At the same time, the head teacher also needs to pay attention to the implementation of the system norms, establishing their own prestige through rewards and punishments, so as to enable students to establish the consciousness of respecting, learning, observing, and using rules. In the specific application, we should do a good job of supervision, through the construction of an orderly class collective system, so as to do a good job in the construction of class system culture. Jin Qing pointed out that the Legalist school advocated "no alienation, no distinction between nobility and inferiority, no break with the law" for the construction of the class system is of great significance. A class is a collective, students should use class rules to restrain their own behavior. Similarly, teachers need to use a fair and just attitude, with a reasonable and scientific system to guide students' behavior habits.[74]

---

[66]Zhong Huijuan. Reflections on Class Management in Universities Based on Traditional Culture [J]. Netizens World, 2012 (14):39–40.

[67]Tan Yinghai. On Class Culture and Its Role in Student Development [J]. Contemporary Education Science, 2003 (10):6–7.

[68]See footnote 66.

[69]Lin Jincai. Class Management [M]. East China Normal University Press, 2006.

[70]Guo Yi. Class Management [M]. People's Education Press, 2002.

[71]See footnote 66.

[72]Gong Qiaoyun. How to Use Traditional Culture for Class Management [J]. Teaching and Management, 2007 (4):17–18.

[73]Lu Xiaoxia. Inheriting National Culture and Shaping Class Spirit [J]. Moral Education in Primary and Secondary Schools, 2008 (8):30–32.

[74]See footnote 47.

7.3 The Counteraction of Class Culture to Traditional Culture

Chinese traditional culture is the soul of the Chinese national spirit. Promoting excellent traditional culture is a strong guarantee for the early realization of the great rejuvenation of the Chinese nation, and it is the most important thing in the field of ideological and cultural construction in the new era. In today's Information Age, how to inherit and develop Chinese traditional culture is worth exploring. Researchers point out that the integration of traditional culture into class culture construction can not only promote the development of class culture but also, in turn, promote the inheritance and development of traditional culture.[75]

Lan Haiyan pointed out that incorporating traditional culture into class culture construction is conducive to enhancing students' understanding of traditional culture and understanding the origin and customs of Chinese traditional culture. For example, the Dragon Boat Festival falls on the fifth day of May every year, but students do not know the lunar calendar. Teachers can improve students' understanding of the lunar calendar through the construction of class culture, to make students understand that the calendar should not only look at the solar calendar but also observe the lunar calendar and understand the culture of our country, which is also conducive to cultivating students' awareness of cultural inheritance.[76] Zou Ke pointed out that Chinese traditional festivals are an important part of Chinese national culture and one of the important carriers to carry forward traditional culture and inherit Chinese virtues. In the construction of class culture, traditional festivals are used as carriers to absorb the cultural elements of traditional festivals so as to enable students to experience the excellent Chinese traditions embodied in traditional festivals, in the process of subtle influence, feel the charm and power of culture.[77] Yu Pan pointed out that the effective combination of traditional culture and class culture is an important way to inherit and develop traditional culture, and an important way to cultivate students' national spirit and national character in the new era.[78]

7.4 Strategies of Class Culture Construction Based on Chinese Traditional Culture

Based on the traditional culture of different schools, the researchers have discussed the strategies of building class culture. Based on Confucianism, researchers put forward the idea of "humanism" and "harmony but difference" into the construction

---

[75] See footnote 52.
[76] See footnote 45.
[77] See footnote 56.
[78] See footnote 46.

of class culture. For example, Lan Haiyan pointed out that humanism is the development and extension of Confucianism. Teachers should adhere to the concept of people-oriented. On the one hand, they should let students participate in the formulation of class rules and regulations, on the other hand, they should let students create class culture by themselves.[79] Xia Tingting proposed that the Confucian "harmony but difference" should be utilized in the course of class construction. Teachers in charge of classes should not only see the consistency of class development, but also allow students to have individual differences, take students' development as the starting point and destination, guide students to establish correct outlook on life, values, and world outlook, and strive to make students form the values of "harmony for truth, harmony for goodness, harmony for beauty, harmony for value," and guide students to correctly handle various interpersonal relationships within the class, to achieve interpersonal harmony and class harmony.[80] Based on the Legalist thought, the researchers also put forward corresponding suggestions on the construction of class culture. For example, Xia Tingting proposed to create a class discipline atmosphere of "rule of law management". In class management, strict class discipline and class rules should be formulated and implemented to promote the formation of a good class atmosphere.[81] Liu Zhiang proposed that we should take the spirit of Legalism as the guidance, strengthen the sense of rules, and let students establish a sense of discipline to form a good class order.[82] Based on Mohist thought, Liu Zhiang also pointed out that the ideas of love, talent appointment, rewards and punishments advocated by the Mohist school can also be used in the construction of class culture. Teachers in charge of classes should treat every student equally, love every student equally; fully exploit the advantages and potentials of students; severely punish violations of discipline, commend achievements and progress, and have clearly reward and punishment.[83]

In the construction of class culture, besides the traditional cultures of different schools, researchers also involved other specific traditional cultures, from which they put forward strategies for the construction of class culture. For example, Lan Haiyan believes that the classics of Chinese classics are the crystallization of ancient sages' thoughts and wisdom in China. In the construction of class culture, teachers should let students recite more classics of Chinese classics and deepen the cultural connotation of the class. Teachers can create calligraphy corners so that students interested in calligraphy can participate in the creation of calligraphy; create music corners so as to let the students who are interested in Chinese classical music appreciate the wonderful music; eight brocade Satin courses are offered to help students interested

---

[79] See footnote 45.

[80] Xia Tingting. Exploration of Integrating Chinese Excellent Traditional Culture into Class Management in Universities [J]. Modernization of Education, 2017, 4 (48):213–214.

[81] See footnote 80.

[82] Li Zhenxing. Life-giving Spring Breeze, Moistening Things Silently—On the Effective Integration of Chinese Traditional Culture in Junior Middle School Class Management [J]. Cultural and educational materials, 2019 (05):157–158.

[83] See footnote 82.

in sports learn how to build up their health, so that students can have a better under-standing of our traditional culture and make the class culture more dense.[84] Tang Fanhong pointed out that classical reading such as "Disciple's Regulation", "Univer-sity", "Doctrine of the Mean" and "Analects" could lead to class culture. Teachers insisted on reading classics together with students every morning, guiding students to understand the main idea of the article, paying attention to emotional experience, and using traditional virtues such as "filial piety, respect, loyalty, credit, etiquette, justice, honesty and shame" to educate students silently; carrying out "moral lecture" as a carrier, fully integrate filial piety into the life of classes, students and parents, and focusing on cultivating students' elegance. We can also combine Qingming, Dragon Boat Festival, Chongyang, Spring Festival, and other traditional Chinese festivals to guide students to understand the knowledge of festival culture, experience the strong atmosphere of the festival, let students experience and feel the national cultural atmosphere hidden in the depth of their thoughts, and cultivate students' feelings of respect and kindness.[85] Yu Ronghua pointed out that the construction of class culture needs the spiritual connotation of continuous self-improvement. We can tell students examples of continuous self-improvement and growth in the classroom to motivate students.[86] Zhang Ying put forward three strategies for the construction of class culture: first, building a "kindness" atmosphere of class culture with the theme of "kindness" and guiding students at four levels: not doing bad things, doing good things, often doing good things, stopping others from doing bad things, and helping them correct. Second, the road is like water, with love as the mainline permeating the concept of "tolerance" of class culture. In the construction of class culture, class teachers and teachers should reach a consensus, truly refer to students as individuals with an independent personality to tolerance and acceptance, and be more patient and tolerant to students. Third, we should cultivate the "eternal" spirit of class culture with guidance as the main factor. In the construction of class culture, we should give priority to guidance, such as water flowing into rivers, and establish an operational system, so as to guide students to start small things, accumulate over time, persevere, and form a diligent and tenacious will.[87] Ding Xiu pointed out that in the construc-tion of class environmental culture, we should pay attention to the excavation of traditional cultural content, strengthen traditional cultural education, let the Chinese traditional culture rooted in the hearts of students, always play a leading, promoting, and stimulating role. First, ancient celebrity portraits, poems, and aphorisms will be added to the corridor walls and updated regularly. The second is to add "Star of Chinese Studies" in the evaluation and demonstration of various models, which will be widely involved in Chinese traditional culture and achieve learning results, and in practice carry forward the traditional virtues of outstanding typical students, judges "Star of Chinese Studies" for recognition and display. The third is to set up exhi-bition corners of excellent traditional culture works on the corridor walls, regularly

---

[84] See footnote 45.

[85] See footnote 49.

[86] See footnote 63.

[87] See footnote 1.

displaying students' Chinese paintings, paper-cut and calligraphy works. Fourth, the column "Learning Ancient Poetry" is set up on the side of the blackboard class newspaper on the back wall of the classroom.[88] Peng Yanghua and others pointed out that excellent traditional culture should be integrated into class culture through text-guided reading. On the one hand, in the form of classes or interest groups, we can sponsor various reading conferences, with classical works of traditional culture as the material, on the other hand, we can systematically invite experts and scholars to give special lectures, we can also establish class patriotism education and traditional culture education bases to give full play to the educational effectiveness of local cultural sites in the times. On major anniversaries and festivals, students are organized to visit bases, study and work voluntarily to enhance their sense of national pride and responsibility of the times.[89]

7.5 Summary

Class culture reflects the mainstream values and ways of doing things of students in a class. Excellent educational ideas, moral education viewpoints, harmonious and friendly spirit, enterprising and realistic class style and civilized etiquette norms in traditional culture are all important aspects of class culture construction. Class culture construction, whether spiritual, institutional, environmental, or behavioral, cannot ignore the excavation and promotion of traditional Chinese culture.

In the context of the rapid development of modern society and culture, it is necessary to carry out the study of class culture construction from the perspective of traditional culture in the class, dig deeply into the resources of traditional culture, carry forward the fine traditional spirit, strengthen traditional culture education, combine traditional culture with class construction, and let students actively carry out the construction of class culture under the bathing of traditional culture, enhance humanistic knowledge, improve their own civilization quality, and increase wisdom. Only by attaching importance to traditional culture, taking traditional culture as the foundation, constructing excellent class culture, cultivating students' socialist core values, cultivating students' core literacy, and making them qualified builders and successors of socialist modernization with Chinese characteristics in the future. Only in this way can we truly fulfill the sacred mission entrusted to us by the Party and the people to cultivate people through virtue.

Through sorting out the literature, we find that the research results on class culture and traditional culture are relatively rich, which lays a foundation for further research on class culture construction from the perspective of traditional culture. However, from the perspective of traditional culture, it lacks the overall framework of integrating traditional culture into class culture and does not form an inherent

---

[88]Ding Xiurong. Traditional Chinese Culture: the Foundation of Class Culture Construction—Practical Exploration of Class Culture Construction [J]. Modern Education Science, 2019 (2):26–29.
[89]See footnote 51.

manifestation; the measures of building class culture around traditional culture are not comprehensive and thorough enough, and further research is needed; in addition, the integration of traditional culture into class culture construction is not only theoretical research. The problems should be effectively carried out in accordance with the actual situation of the school.

CPSIA information can be obtained
at www.ICGtesting.com
Printed in the USA
LVHW052313141220
674148LV00005B/362

9 789811 518294